The Solitary Auditor

The Solitary Auditor

Michael Chris Knapp
UNIVERSITY OF OKLAHOMA

CAROLINA ACADEMIC PRESS
Durham, North Carolina

Library of Congress Cataloging-in-Publication Data

Names: Knapp, Michael Chris, 1954- author.
Title: The solitary auditor / Michael C. Knapp.
Description: Durham, North Carolina : Carolina Academic Press, [2016] |
   Includes bibliographical references and index.
Identifiers: LCCN 2016002659 | ISBN 9781611638783 (alk. paper)
Subjects: LCSH: Auditing. | Corporations--Auditing.
Classification: LCC HF5667 .K5324 2016 | DDC 657/.45--dc23
LC record available at http://lccn.loc.gov/2016002659

CAROLINA ACADEMIC PRESS, LLC
700 Kent Street
Durham, North Carolina 27701
Telephone (919) 489-7486
Fax (919) 493-5668
www.cap-press.com

Printed in the United States of America
2018 Printing

Contents

Preface

Since Congress passed the federal securities laws in the early 1930s, independent auditors have served as the appointed watchdogs for our nation's capital markets. The investing and lending public trusts auditors to pierce the veil of secrecy surrounding modern corporations and ferret out window-dressed financial statements intended to dupe the unsuspecting. Unfortunately, the long roll call of financial scandals that includes Enron, WorldCom, Madoff Securities, and Lehman Brothers, among many others, suggests that trust has often been misplaced. Each successive scandal imposed multi-billion dollar losses on investors, further undercut the public's confidence in our nation's capital markets, and raised increasing levels of doubt regarding the competence and diligence of independent auditors.

Just as damaging to the psyche of the investing public has been the litany of insider trading scandals that have rocked Wall Street in recent years. Shockingly, several of those scandals have involved independent auditors, including the vice chairman of a Big Four accounting firm. In another case, the FBI captured on videotape a senior partner in the West Coast audit practice of another Big Four firm accepting bricks of $100 bills in payment for confidential information that he had given to a golfing buddy. The prison sentences handed down to those partners by the federal courts did nothing to salvage the investing public's trust in the integrity of independent auditors.

Before identifying measures to strengthen the independent audit function and enhance its credibility, it is first imperative that we better understand the pressure-packed and secretive work environment of independent auditors. *The Solitary Auditor* pulls back the curtains on that shadowy work environment and reveals the inner workings of independent audits and the circumstances that often diminish, if not destroy, the quality and usefulness of those audits. Although a fictional work, the storyline of *The Solitary Auditor* relies almost exclusively on specific circumstances and events drawn from the hundreds of problem audits and audit failures that I have spent 35 years studying and documenting in my academic career.

The Solitary Auditor storyline revolves around a newly-minted audit senior, Michael Bishop, who learns that his client's senior executives have engineered an elaborate accounting fraud to boost their company's reported revenues and profits. To save the jobs, if not careers, of the senior BRIC accountants who have been browbeaten into participating in the fraud, Bishop agrees to cooperate with a plan developed by those accountants to end the fraud. But the plan backfires and Bishop becomes a pawn in a three-handed cat-and-mouse game involving the fraudsters, federal law enforcement authorities, and a shadowy syndicate of inside traders who intend to make a "killing" in the stock market when the accounting fraud is exposed.

Michael C. Knapp
David Ross Boyd Professor
McLaughlin Chair in Business Ethics
Professor of Accounting
University of Oklahoma

The Solitary Auditor

Chapter 1

Tuesday, October 15

"We are going to be spending a lot of time together, Michael, so I think we need to make the best of it." There was an underlying tone of parental condescension in Emma Nelson's voice as she spoke to her subordinate.

Michael Bishop, who was sitting across from Nelson at the oversized conference table, shrugged his shoulders in a show of disinterest. "Okay. Whatever you say."

"That's real encouraging," Nelson responded sarcastically.

Bishop straightened up in his chair and faced Nelson squarely. "Emma, I'm just your assistant on this job. Once you give me some paper-shuffling assignments, I will immediately get to work on them. What more do you expect from me?"

"I was expecting that you would have enough professional courtesy and respect to at least pretend to be interested in this audit." Frustrated and angry, Nelson shook her head in disgust. "You are an audit senior, too, you know."

"Yeah, but you're the 'supervising' audit senior on this job, Emma. I'm just your flunky."

Nelson and Bishop shared the same start date with their employer, a large Midwestern practice office of a Big Four accounting firm. But Nelson had been promoted to audit senior after only two years with the firm, while Bishop had spent more than three years with the firm before receiving his promotion to audit senior—his promotion had become effective only two weeks earlier on October 1.

"Okay, I am going to print out a few more work papers from the permanent file," Nelson said as she began taking out her anger on the keyboard of her laptop computer. "There. Done. Now, I'm going to pick up these work papers. When I return, I want to begin by giving you an overview of BRIC, its management team, its industry, and its recent financial performance. After that, I will discuss recent audits of the company and some of the key issues that we may face on this year's audit." Nelson stood, adjusted a wayward curl that had been bungee jumping down the middle of her forehead, and then stomped out of the conference room.

3

Emma Nelson and Michael Bishop were having their initial planning meeting for the year-end audit of BRIC Industries, a large manufacturing company whose common stock was traded on the New York Stock Exchange. Nelson would be the supervising audit senior, while Bishop would be serving as her principal assistant on the engagement. Nelson was the only returning member of the BRIC audit engagement team—this would be the fourth year she had participated in the audit of the company whose fiscal year coincided with the calendar year. Throughout the previous six months, Nelson had done some limited planning for the audit, but this was the first planning meeting for the engagement and it was not going well.

Given the turnover on the BRIC engagement team, the responsibility for servicing the client during the past few months, including most of the work in reviewing the client's quarterly 10-Q reports filed with the SEC, had fallen on Nelson's shoulders. Early in the prior week, Nelson had received an email indicating that Cason Kellis and Jim Wilmeth would be serving as the audit engagement partner and audit manager, respectively, for the BRIC audit. Nelson told Bishop that she immediately sent each of them an email "notifying" them of the initial audit planning meeting, but neither had responded to those emails— Bishop had never been assigned to an engagement on which an audit senior scheduled the planning meetings.

Unknown to Nelson, neither Kellis nor Wilmeth wanted to be assigned to the BRIC engagement, which explained why they hadn't responded to her emails. The audit partner and audit manager previously assigned to the BRIC audit team had been given other assignments for the upcoming busy season. Because of a critical staffing shortage in the practice office, there was no one else available to serve as the audit engagement partner and audit manager for the BRIC engagement. In fact, by the end of the day, Todd Wilson, the office managing partner (OMP), would deny for the second time the requests of Kellis and Wilmeth to be scratched from the BRIC audit team and order each of them to contact Emma Nelson. Wilson was concerned because the planning for the large BRIC audit was well behind schedule.

Unlike Kellis and Wilmeth, Emma Nelson was unaware that BRIC Industries ranked as one of the least desirable audit clients of their practice office, which employed several hundred audit professionals. Given the company's size, Nelson viewed the BRIC engagement as a coveted assignment and one that would enhance her goal of being promoted as quickly as possible to audit manager.

Bishop's assignment to the BRIC audit team had been unwelcome news for Nelson because he had a reputation as a slacker within their office. Nelson didn't have any firsthand knowledge of Bishop's work ethic since they had never been assigned to the same engagement, but she was acquainted with him because some three years earlier they had attended the same two-week training session for newly hired staff accountants.

The two audit seniors had little in common when it came to their backgrounds and personalities. Nelson, an only child whose parents were a prominent trial attorney and an orthodontist, was an outgoing, spontaneous, and attractive young lady with curly shoulder-length blonde hair. In the office, she had a reputation as a fashion plate among her peers because of her large wardrobe of stylish business attire.

Nelson was also ambitious, hard-working, and hypercompetitive. Some of her coworkers privately viewed her as overly self-assured, if not downright cocky. Those who were most critical of her suggested that she routinely "sucked up" to individuals in positions of authority. "How is this decision going to affect how I am perceived by my superiors?" was the question that seemed to dictate her behavior in any given context.

Despite Nelson's apparent self-confidence, she often wrestled with self-doubt. She frequently felt that she was "over her head" on difficult assignments involving complex accounting issues. On evenings and weekends, Nelson sometimes spent long hours researching such issues, chargeable hours that she didn't include in her weekly time reports.

In contrast to Nelson, Bishop had been raised with his younger sister Jessica in a single-parent household by their mother who was an elementary school teacher. He was quiet and serious, some would say somber. Tall and handsome, Bishop had a tan complexion and jet-black hair thanks to his Native American heritage—his maternal grandmother was a full-blooded Rosebud Sioux. A childhood accident had left Bishop with a three-inch scar that extended diagonally from under his left eye to the bridge of his nose. The facial scar didn't detract from his good looks, but it did give him a somewhat sinister appearance when coupled with the fact that he seldom smiled.

Although labeled as a slacker by the office's clique of fast-track seniors— Emma Nelson was a charter member of that group—Bishop wasn't lazy. He participated in all office functions, was never late for work, and completed his assignments competently and on a timely basis. Unlike Nelson who had retaken two sections of the CPA exam before earning her certificate, Bishop had passed all four parts of the exam on his first attempt. And, despite his sullen appearance, coworkers who had taken the time and effort to get to know Bishop found him to be pleasant and accommodating and generous with his time when asked for help. He was articulate and more than willing to engage in conversation in a social context as long as the topic of conversation didn't involve him. Bishop was intensely private; he respected the privacy of his coworkers and expected them to reciprocate.

Bishop had been labeled as a slacker by the office's fast-track seniors because, unlike each of them, he refused to "go the extra mile." He didn't exhibit the unbridled energy, enthusiasm, and take charge leadership skills that were mandatory personality traits for individuals who had chosen to pursue the fast track to partnership. Rather than tackling his assignments with energy and enthusiasm similar to Nelson, Bishop typically exhibited no more than a lukewarm interest in them. That lackadaisical attitude caused his superiors to downgrade his otherwise strong performance on his assignments.

The day before their initial planning meeting for the BRIC audit, Nelson had invited Bishop to go to lunch with her. Nelson had intended to use the lunch to get to know Bishop better and to assure him that they could work well together as a team. Unfortunately, the lunch was less than productive. Nelson tried her best to get Bishop to open up to her, but the only personal information she gleaned from their conversation was that his home was somewhere in southern California, a four-hour airplane flight from the metropolitan area in which they worked, and the fact that he was two years older than her.

After learning Bishop's age, Nelson had tried to inject a little levity into their conversation by suggesting that it must have taken him seven years to complete his five-year accounting program. That lighthearted statement had been met with icy silence from Bishop who didn't want anyone prying into his personal background. Unknown to Nelson, Bishop had asked to be assigned to a practice office of his employer that was far from his home to minimize the chance that any of his coworkers would know him.

Nelson realized that most professionals would consider Bishop's assignment on the BRIC engagement as her subordinate demeaning since he was at the same employment rank as her and had the same amount of public accounting experience. She assumed that was the principal source of the tension between the two of them. She also assumed that Bishop didn't like her because she was widely perceived as the star of their start class. Because of the very competitive work environment of the major accounting firms, it was difficult for individuals at the same employment level in a practice office to be friends. At least that had been Nelson's experience.

Bishop was actually happy that Nelson would be serving as the principal supervisor of the BRIC audit fieldwork. Because Nelson was a high-strung workaholic who took every opportunity to impress her superiors, Bishop assumed that she would insist on overseeing every facet of the engagement. That meant he would most likely wind up functioning as an experienced staff accountant, a role that he had become comfortable with before being promoted to audit senior.

Nelson was also wrong about Bishop's attitude toward her. He did not dislike her and he didn't resent her for choosing to pursue the fast track to partnership. He respected her decision to pursue that career path, but it was not a career path that he envisioned for himself.

Unlike Nelson, Bishop didn't have any definite career goals. For the time being, he just wanted to survive in the cutthroat, up-or-out work environment of Big Four public accounting. He was relieved that he finally had been promoted to audit senior, otherwise he would have been "counseled out" of the firm, a nice way of saying "fired."

Bishop realized that Nelson viewed the BRIC audit engagement as a vehicle to embellish her already sterling image in their practice office. She desperately wanted the audit to succeed because of the large measure of responsibility she had been given for the engagement. Bishop, on the other hand, viewed the BRIC audit as just another assignment and had no intention of making the success of the engagement a personal priority for him.

"Okay, let's get this started," Nelson said with a grim tone of determination in her voice as she sat back down at the conference room table after returning with two stacks of documents. "I printed out two copies of each of these items. Here's your file," she added as she slid a sheaf of documents across the table in Bishop's direction.

Nelson began by reviewing BRIC's history and operations. In terms of total revenues and market capitalization, BRIC was one of the 300 largest public companies in the United States. The manufacturing company, which was organized by product line into four divisions, had grown rapidly after it was founded during World War II. But, by the turn of the century, several new competitors had begun eroding BRIC's market share and adversely impacting the company's profit margins.

Three years earlier, BRIC's board of directors had cleaned house by hiring a new chief executive officer (CEO), chief operating officer (COO), and chief financial officer (CFO) who were charged with turning around the company. The new executives appeared to have accomplished that goal. They had done an especially noteworthy job of enhancing BRIC's image within the investment community. BRIC's public relations department frequently issued press releases that touted new joint ventures, new marketing programs, and other positive developments involving the company.

Since the hiring of the new management team, several of BRIC's key operating measures had steadily improved. The company had reported increased revenues during each of the previous twelve quarterly reporting periods, a remarkable achievement given the weak national economy over that time frame. BRIC's key profitability ratios now compared favorably with the same ratios of the four companies that were considered to be its peer group. Unlike BRIC, those companies' operating results had faltered as the national economy weakened.

As Nelson continued her review of BRIC's recent financial performance, the story she was weaving seemed implausible to Bishop. There seemed to be an obvious disconnect between BRIC's improving profitability over the past few years and the reality of the competitive conditions that it faced. Bishop wondered how the company had increased its revenues and profits in the face of a weak national economy while the financial performance of its principal competitors had steadily worsened. That result seemed particularly implausible since those competitors had more modern and efficient manufacturing and distribution facilities than BRIC.

There were other red flags that also caught Bishop's attention. Despite the improvement in its profitability ratios, Bishop noticed that the quality of BRIC's earnings, as measured by the relationship between net operating cash flows and net income, had gradually declined over the past three years. Likewise, several of the company's key asset management ratios, including its receivables and inventory turnover ratios, had also deteriorated over that time span.

Nelson seemed oblivious to the warning signs evident in BRIC Industries' recent history and financial data. At one point during her overview of the company, she commented on the "superb" management skills of its three top executives. She then noted matter-of-factly that the previous management team "clearly didn't have a clue" and that the company's stockholders should be very grateful that BRIC's board had brought in a team of skilled turnaround specialists to run the company. The successful turnaround of the company had caught the attention of third parties. According to Nelson, rumors had been circulating over the past few months that a large private equity fund was targeting BRIC as a takeover candidate. If those rumors were true, the equity fund intended to buy BRIC's outstanding common stock and take the company private.

A possible explanation for BRIC's apparent turnaround, in Bishop's mind, was creative accounting schemes orchestrated by the new management team. The growing roll call of financial reporting scandals in years past had convinced Bishop that many corporate executives were self-interested miscreants who sculpted their companies' reported operating results to achieve their personal goals.

Bishop would later learn that there were more tangible reasons to question BRIC's dramatic turnaround. For example, the company's new management team had slashed BRIC's research and development budget to improve the company's operating results. Instead of relying on its own research and development activities, BRIC was forced to mimic the new business strategies and products introduced by its competitors. The new executives had also made large cuts in discretionary expenditures necessary to maintain the company's production facilities in top operating condition. Several of BRIC's factories were becoming obsolete and the cuts in the repairs and maintenance budget for those facilities were exacerbating that problem. In fact, BRIC's anemic operating cash flows limited management's ability to undertake major strategic initiatives such as modernizing its production facilities.

After completing her report on BRIC's recent financial performance, Emma Nelson transitioned to an overview of the company's recent audits. Nelson told Bishop that BRIC's senior financial executives didn't "require significant interaction with the audit team." The offices of the company's CFO and corporate controller were considered off limits to the auditors performing the fieldwork for the engagement. Only the audit engagement partner was allowed to speak to those two individuals.

The auditors' liaison with BRIC's management team was the company's general accounting manager, William "Bud" Wallace, who was also the principal decision maker when it came to important accounting and financial reporting matters. The tone of Nelson's voice when she mentioned Wallace's name signaled that she had little respect for him. Nelson showed some surprising, if modest, insight when she observed that, "It's strange that such a large company allows a glorified accounting clerk to make all major accounting and financial reporting decisions."

By this point, Bishop had decided that BRIC's management team likely viewed its company's annual audit as a necessary evil. It was also apparent that the company's accounting and financial reporting function and internal control system were not priorities for its executives. Those conclusions prompted another shrewd and accurate observation on Bishop's part: Cason Kellis and Jim Wilmeth were probably doing everything possible to get themselves removed from the high-risk and career-threatening BRIC audit engagement, which explained why they had not responded to Nelson's emails.

As Nelson droned on and on, it became apparent to Bishop that, despite her frustration at being unable to initiate any dialogue with Kellis or Wilmeth, she clearly relished the fact that she was effectively overseeing the audit of a large public company. It seemed more than a little odd to Bishop that Nelson was filling that role, if only temporarily. Here was a company whose market value was measured in the billions of dollars and yet the principal guardian of the investing and lending public's interest in that entity was a relatively inexperienced, if not airheaded, audit senior.

"Well, that's my 'state of the audit' speech for BRIC Industries," Nelson announced. Upon glancing at her Rolex, Nelson added, "Wow, I can't believe that I've been talking for so long."

Nelson's extended monologue had caused her anger and frustration to dissipate.

"Michael, do you have any questions?" she asked cheerily.

Bishop shifted his weight in his chair and then cleared his throat before responding. "Uh, no. That's a, uh, uh, pretty comprehensive overview. So ... thorough, matter of fact, that I don't have any questions."

Nelson took Bishop's completely insincere statement as a sincere compliment. "Well, thank you, Michael. I really appreciate it." Nelson then told Bishop that she would pay a visit to Kellis's office if he or Wilmeth didn't respond within the next day or two to her earlier e-mails and that she would contact Bishop as soon as she obtained a better understanding of the timeline for the BRIC audit.

After he and Nelson said their good-byes, Bishop resolved to make the best of his time on the BRIC audit engagement. He realized that working for the pretentious and overbearing Nelson would pose some challenges for him, including dealing with Nelson's naive attitude toward the role of independent auditors and the overall nature of independent auditing.

As a result of their lunch meeting the previous day and the tedious planning meeting that had just concluded, Bishop had come to understand that he and Nelson had diametrically opposed mindsets when it came to auditing. Nelson believed that most business people were scrupulously honest. During their lunch, she had mentioned to Bishop that if she spent her entire career in public accounting, she doubted that she would encounter more than a handful of situations involving fraud or other dishonest conduct. She noted that although professional standards "force" auditors to spend considerable time searching for fraud, in her opinion, auditors' primary role was to "clean up" after their clients. Auditors pointed out honest mistakes and errors made by clients and helped them strengthen their accounting, control, and financial reporting functions.

Unlike Nelson, Bishop had little respect for the independent audit function—a point of view that he hadn't shared and didn't plan to share with Nelson. Bishop privately held his employer and its audit partners in contempt. Rather than being objective financial detectives, Bishop had come to believe that most audit partners wanted their subordinates to cater to the demands of their clients and pay little or no attention to the fact that they were supposed to be serving as watchdogs for the investing and lending public.

Bishop was convinced that the last thing that audit partners wanted their subordinates to find were errors, intentional or otherwise, in a client's accounting records. Such errors only served to complicate the life of an audit partner. Instead of performing rigorous audits of their clients, the typical audit partner wanted to complete each engagement as quickly, quietly, and politely as possible and then move on to the next audit. Rather than being objective-minded referees, audit partners spent most of their time schmoozing with, and otherwise ingratiating themselves to, client executives.

Within a year of going to work in public accounting, Bishop had decided that most audit partners were not skilled technicians but rather rainmakers who were marketing experts. Those individuals who had the appropriate skeptical mindset and technical skills to carry out the profession's watchdog role likely became frustrated and left public accounting after a few years when they recognized that they were underappreciated by their employers. The result was a race to the bottom in terms of audit quality for the auditing profession.

The futility of independent audits was readily affirmed, in Bishop's mind, by the frequent audit failures reported by the business press. He was perplexed that legislative and regulatory authorities didn't take more aggressive steps to strengthen independent audits. When those parties did act, the resulting measures were typically band-aid type remedies that proved to be largely ineffective.

Bishop believed that the Big Four firms perpetuated the problems inherent in the independent audit function by lobbying against proposals, such as mandatory audit firm rotation, that would likely strengthen independent audits. Instead of serving as advocates for the public interest, Bishop privately saw the Big Four firms as well-oiled propaganda machines that had created a public image for themselves totally different from their actual cultures. The firms seemed more dedicated to increasing their market share of public company audits and cultivating other revenue streams than protecting the millions of investors, lenders, and other third parties that relied on them as the final line of defense against crooked corporate executives.

The young CPA also resented the major accounting firms for overworking and underpaying lower-level employees, such as himself. To Bishop it was laughable that the Big Four firms regularly appeared on Top 100 lists of the nation's best employers. He suspected that the organizations appearing on those lists somehow manipulated their reported employment data or otherwise defeated the notoriously unreliable survey research methods used to collect that data.

Because Bishop realized that most of his coworkers, especially his superiors, would not find his attitudes toward the independent audit function, Big Four firms, and corporate executives palatable, he kept those opinions to himself. Surprisingly, Bishop had an accurate, and less than positive, view of his own suitability for the role of independent auditor. He recognized that he was an underachiever—at least the way that term was defined by individuals such as Emma Nelson—and that he was definitely a malcontent whose negative attitudes toward the auditing discipline were likely related to his failure to advance rapidly within his firm. He also admitted to himself that he had no interest in working toward improving independent audits because that would require him to make a sizable commitment of energy and emotion.

Instead of "taking on city hall," Bishop was more than willing to linger on the periphery of the auditing discipline and privately berate it. He realized that within a few years he would almost certainly be told by his superiors that he wasn't cut out for public accounting and would be forced to find another job.

In the meantime, Bishop planned to remain in public accounting as long as he could. Why? Because strangely enough, he enjoyed his work. Performing an audit was somewhat like playing a game. There were rules, there was structure, there were opposing parties, and there was an outcome. And, despite resenting his employer for the large amount of overtime that he worked, he preferred ticking and tying, chasing down client documents, and clearing review comments to staying home in his apartment where his principal forms of entertainment were Netflix videos and Sudoku puzzles.

Chapter 2

Monday, October 28

"Welcome everyone. I am glad you could make it. We all have busy schedules, so I want to keep this meeting as brief as possible." Cason Kellis paused as he gathered up the attention of the dozen or so individuals in BRIC Industries' corporate boardroom. "As most of you know, I have been given the great honor of overseeing the BRIC Industries audit this year. Unfortunately for you, Lonnie Grigsby could not return to head up the audit team because he has been given a couple of major assignments that conflict with the timing of the BRIC Industries audit. So ... I guess you're stuck with me," Kellis added with a forced smile as he poked his arms in the air as if he was a referee signaling a touchdown.

The partner's weak attempt at humor sparked only a couple of modest chuckles from his captive audience. "By the way," Kellis continued, "Lonnie told me to send his regards. Now, let's get to the matter at hand."

Michael Bishop barely stifled a laugh as he watched Kellis struggle to appear as if he was happy to be serving as the BRIC audit engagement partner. By this time, Bishop had learned that Grigsby, the former BRIC audit engagement partner, had asked to be transferred to another office if he wasn't taken off the BRIC job, while Kellis had sparred tooth and nail with Todd Wilson, the OMP, when he had been tabbed to take Grigsby's place.

Bishop had also learned why BRIC Industries was considered a particularly loathsome audit client. The company's senior management team was reportedly difficult, if not impossible, to deal with when problematic accounting or financial reporting issues arose during an audit. BRIC's management played a tough game of poker in which they continually bluffed the auditors: "Accept our resolution of the issue you raised or resign and, in doing so, forfeit the multimillion dollar fee that you are paid every year for this engagement." The apparently conscientious Lonnie Grigsby had tired of the poker game and insisted on being replaced as the audit engagement partner.

After a few more welcoming remarks, Kellis asked the individuals present to briefly introduce themselves. Kellis had called the meeting to allow key members of the BRIC audit team to meet the client personnel they would be working with during the upcoming audit.

In addition to Kellis and Bishop, the members of the audit team present included Emma Nelson and Jim Wilmeth. Client personnel present included Suzanne Jennings, the company's CFO; Jameson Hardy, the corporate controller; and Bud Wallace, the general accounting manager. Also present were the director of the company's internal audit department and the controller of each of BRIC's four divisions, three of whom had been with the company for approximately two years. The controller of BRIC's largest division had been on the job for 18 months.

Bishop would later learn that within her first year at BRIC Industries Jennings had replaced all four divisional controllers because she wanted to put her "own people" in place. After she hired a new controller for BRIC's largest division that individual had resigned several months later forcing Jennings to replace him. No one knew how Wallace, who had joined BRIC a few months before Jennings arrived, had survived the overhaul of the company's accounting staff.

"Now, I would like to turn the floor over to Suzanne. I appreciate her taking the time to stop by and say 'hello' to the members of the green visor brigade." Kellis's second weak attempt at humor drew no reaction from Jennings who was sitting at the head of the conference room table to Kellis's immediate right. The sharply-dressed and stern-faced CFO made no effort to conceal the fact that she had much more important things to do than engage in small talk with a gaggle of bean counters.

Although the 45-year-old Jennings headed up BRIC's financial management team, she had only limited formal training in finance and accounting. She had earned an undergraduate degree in history from one of the Seven Sisters, the loose association of prestigious East Coast liberal arts colleges that cater primarily to women. After three years working in an entry-level position at a major public relations firm in New York City, Jennings had enrolled in an Ivy League MBA program. Following the completion of her MBA degree, she had spent the next 15 years working with a leading East Coast consulting firm. Mergers and acquisitions had been her area of specialization.

Jennings had been persuaded to accept the CFO position at BRIC Industries by two former colleagues of hers at the consulting firm. Those two individuals, Samuel Duncan Hakes, IV, and Vaughn Jeffrey "Jett" Zimmer, were chosen to serve as the company's new CEO and COO, respectively, when BRIC's board of directors decided three years earlier that the company needed a new management team.

"Thank you, Cason," Jennings said almost politely as she stood to address those present. "I have a conference call later this morning with several securities analysts, so I will be leaving after I make a few comments."

Before continuing, Jennings crossed her arms and then turned to face Kellis and his three colleagues sitting on the left side of the conference room table.

"As we all know, public companies are required to have their annual financial statements audited before those statements can be filed with the SEC. I point that out because I want each of you to realize that archaic requirement is the only reason you are here." The brash statement and the contemptuous tone of Jennings' voice made Cason Kellis flinch noticeably. "Independent audits may be necessary for some companies," Jennings continued, "but at BRIC Industries we have a state-of-the-art accounting and management information system and a staff of expert accountants and I.T. professionals that make your services redundant. Our thorough system of internal checks and balances ensure that any errors in our accounting records that happen to occur are quickly identified and corrected."

Jennings turned her back to the auditors briefly like a gunfighter reloading his six-shooter. Then, she wheeled and took aim once more at the four sitting ducks.

"I always take it as a personal affront when auditors ask pointed questions to my subordinates about potential fraud. I can assure you that you will not find an organization, including your own, that has a stronger, more comprehensive, and more vigorously enforced code of ethics than BRIC Industries."

Jennings slowly slid her piercing gaze down the row of auditors to make sure that each of them was hanging on her every word.

"I realize that you have a job to do and my staff will assist you in completing your tests when necessary, but I want you to understand that we have our own jobs to do. And our jobs do not involve training the pack of inquisitive, newly hired staff accountants that you send to our headquarters office each year."

Jennings made eye-to-eye contact with Cason Kellis. It was obvious that she had no intention of continuing until Kellis acknowledged her previous comment.

After a few awkward moments, Kellis cleared his throat and nodded vigorously like a six-year-old child who had just been dressed down by his mother.

"Mr. Wallace," Jennings said as she motioned with her right hand to the other side of the table while keeping her eyes trained on the four auditors, "will serve as the liaison between the company and your team. Funnel any requests for information through him and his immediate subordinates." Jennings uncrossed her arms and then stepped toward the open door of the conference room. At first, it appeared that she intended to leave the room without saying anything else. But then, she added, almost courteously, "Thank you and good luck," before marching out of the room.

After Jennings left, Michael Bishop glanced at his three colleagues sitting to his right. "Why me" expressions were evident on the faces of Kellis and Wilmeth. Emma Nelson, on the other hand, had a look of starstruck admiration on her face.

As he stepped back to the head of the conference room table, Cason Kellis fidgeted with his bow tie as he attempted to regain his composure—Kellis always wore a bow tie rather than a necktie when he was dressed in a business suit, apparently that was his signature fashion statement. After a few general comments regarding the audit, Kellis asked Emma Nelson to provide an overview of the timeline for the engagement.

For the next 15 minutes, Nelson, who was resplendent in a burgundy pinstriped business suit accented by a shockingly yellow ruffled silk shirt, waltzed her way through a series of PowerPoint slides that identified the key dates in the audit, the documents that would be requested by the auditors, and other assistance that the audit team would need from client personnel. Throughout her presentation, Nelson rarely looked at anyone other than Cason Kellis. As Michael Bishop sat watching Nelson, he got the impression that she was a Miss America candidate and that Cason Kellis was the sole judge of the beauty pageant.

The BRIC accountants who lined the other side of the table paid respectful attention to Nelson's presentation with the exception of Jameson Hardy, the heavyset and silver-haired corporate controller. On multiple occasions, Hardy nodded off only to be rudely awakened when his chin bounced off his chest.

Bishop would later learn that no one, including the senior members of BRIC's accounting staff, knew exactly what Hardy did each day that he spent in his office. Two or three days per week, Hardy would show up at BRIC's headquarters and then spend five to six hours sequestered in his office before leaving. He spent the rest of the week either on a golf course or in the bar of a nearby country club.

To say that Hardy was out of the loop when it came to BRIC's top management was a gross understatement. The only reason the sixty-something senior citizen kept his job was the fact that he was the grandson of the company's founder and served as the managing officer of a family trust that controlled 12 percent of BRIC's outstanding common stock.

When Emma Nelson asked at the conclusion of her presentation if there were any questions, the only individual who responded was Bud Wallace, the general accounting manager. Wallace attempted to show some degree of interest by asking Nelson a few softball questions for which he, no doubt, already knew the answers.

Nelson used each of Wallace's questions as an opportunity to revisit one or more of her burgundy and yellow-hued PowerPoint slides. It was the first time that Bishop had witnessed a presentation in which the presenter had coordinated his or her outfit with the color scheme of the given PowerPoint slides.

After Nelson thoroughly answered the final question posed by Wallace, Cason Kellis asked Jim Wilmeth to discuss specific challenges that the audit team expected to encounter during the BRIC Industries engagement. As Wilmeth made his way to the head of the table, Bishop wondered why the audit team would alert the client's accounting staff to such matters. Given the "let's work together" mantra being espoused by Kellis, Bishop half expected Wilmeth to pull up last year's audit program on the computer screen and walk through it for the benefit of Wallace & Company.

Bishop had not previously worked on an engagement with Cason Kellis, but he had spent a few weeks one summer assigned to the audit of a local not-for-profit organization supervised by Jim Wilmeth. The sum total of Bishop's interaction with Wilmeth had consisted of a couple of lunches attended by the three other members of that audit team and an hour or so discussing Wilmeth's review comments on work papers that Bishop had prepared.

Unlike Kellis, Wilmeth was not flamboyant or superficial. Wilmeth was a classic example of a Big Four audit manager who had no hope of advancing to partner. Bishop wasn't sure how long Wilmeth had been with the firm, but he was certain that the audit manager had at most a few years remaining before he was banished to the private sector.

Instead of a rainmaker, à la Cason Kellis, Jim Wilmeth was a technician. Sadly enough, Wilmeth could quote critical passages from both the accounting and auditing standards. In addition to being extremely bright and articulate, Wilmeth was imprudent, insensitive, and perpetually disheveled in appearance.

Wilmeth frequently sprinkled off-color jokes and sexual innuendos into dialogue with his subordinates. Bishop hadn't been offended by Wilmeth's brutish behavior during the not-for-profit audit, but the uncouth audit manager had made the two female staff accountants assigned to that engagement extremely uncomfortable.

There was no doubt in Bishop's mind that Wilmeth's coarse manners would clash with the pretentious disposition of Emma Nelson. Bishop smiled inwardly when the thought occurred to him that over the next few months he would have front row tickets each day to a brand new reality show: "Jim & Emma at the BRIC." The show might not rival the Kardashians for entertainment value, but it would certainly provide a diversion from the mundane world of file cabinets, subsidiary ledgers, and electronic work papers.

––––––––––

After the meeting with the client personnel ended, Cason Kellis invited his three subordinates to have lunch with him at a nearby French brasserie. Michael Bishop assumed that Kellis would spend much of the informal lunch meeting discussing the raging impertinence of Suzanne Jennings. Surprisingly, Kellis never mentioned her or referred to the brash statements she had made. Instead, he spent most of the lunch telling his three subordinates how "extremely busy" he was going to be over the next several months, which was his way of letting them know that he was going to do as little as possible on the BRIC audit.

Although Kellis was an audit partner, he spent considerable time working with the large in-house group of business consultants assigned to his practice office. The consulting group often used Kellis as their marketing "pitch man." Once a proposal for a large consulting project was complete, Kellis would step in and help develop a presentation that he would then deliver to the prospective client with evangelistic zeal.

The proposed projects were typically multimillion-dollar engagements that were being hawked to non-audit clients given the constraints that the Sarbanes-Oxley Act imposed on the provision of consulting services to audit clients. Then again, Kellis reportedly never missed an opportunity to market consulting projects to his audit clients as well. More often than not, those projects skirted the outer limits of what was considered acceptable consulting services for audit firms to provide to their public company audit clients.

Another project that consumed much of Kellis's time and attention was an initiative that had been launched at the beginning of the year to develop a biotech specialization within his practice office. Over the past decade, the greater metropolitan area where that practice office was located had become a magnet for biotech start-ups, particularly biopharmaceutical companies. Todd Wilson had brought in several consultants with biotech backgrounds to help recruit such companies as clients, but Kellis was spearheading that effort.

To date, Kellis had only landed three small biotech companies as audit clients, but he was targeting two of the largest biopharmaceutical firms in the metro area, both of which were public companies. If Kellis was successful in recruiting those firms, rumors were that the practice office would officially create a biotech industry service team that Kellis would head up. Bishop was aware that several of the ambitious, fast-track staffers in the office were desperate to join that team once it was formed. There was little doubt in Bishop's mind that Emma Nelson's efforts to curry favor with Kellis were related to her desire to be a member of that team.

Midway through the lunch at the French brasserie, Kellis turned to Jim Wilmeth and asked him to provide an overview of the proposed staffing for the BRIC audit. Wilmeth didn't respond immediately, choosing instead to take another bite of his croissant sandwich. After washing down the bite with some raspberry-spiked tea, Wilmeth shrugged and then finally spoke.

"Well, Cason, I don't know any more than you do about the staffing for the BRIC audit. No one has told me anything and, quite frankly, I haven't had time to ask. I've been working like a dog on the audit plan for the new hospital client that we just picked up. Like I told you several days ago, I'll be spending a lot of my time on that job over the next few months."

Kellis laughed heartily and then shook his head before turning to Emma Nelson. "Well, Emma, congratulations," he said with a cheery but sarcastic tone to his voice. "Looks like you're going to be running the BRIC audit pretty much on your own."

Before Kellis could continue, Nelson responded with an enthusiastic, "Wow, I can't wait to get started."

Kellis laughed again as he patted Nelson on the shoulder. "Okay, Emma, I'm just kidding. Although we are both very busy and weren't expecting to have the BRIC engagement fall into our laps, Jim and I are going to make sure that this is a successful audit. But the two of us are going to be forced to rely real heavily on you during this job." Kellis placed his right hand on Nelson's left hand as it was resting on the table top. "I just want you to know that we are very lucky to have the best audit senior in the entire office assigned to supervise the fieldwork on this job."

Nelson beamed as she stared starry-eyed at Kellis. "Sir, I am going to do everything possible to make sure that I earn that praise and—"

"Wait a minute, wait a minute, young lady," Kellis said, interrupting Nelson. "Let's get this straight. I am not a 'sir.' I'm 'Cason.' We are going to be on a first-name basis. Understand? I want you to put me on your favorites list on your cell phone. And I am going to do the same for you."

Bishop expected Kellis to reach over and kiss Nelson on the cheek, if not the lips. Instead, Kellis leaned over and wrapped his right arm around Nelson's shoulders as she fought to hold back tears.

As Kellis was preoccupied with mugging Nelson, Wilmeth turned to Bishop and inserted his left index finger into his mouth prompting a pseudo gag reflex.

Chapter 3

Thursday, October 31

In years past, Michael Bishop had heard stories of the lively and lavish Halloween party hosted each year by Cason Kellis at his sprawling suburban home. Given the huge size of Kellis's practice office, he limited the invitation list to the audit partners in the office, key administrative personnel, and the audit professionals assigned to the engagements that he supervised. Because the stars had aligned and landed both Kellis and Bishop on the BRIC Industries engagement, Bishop was invited to this year's party. Bishop went to the party solo although the RSVP invitation had encouraged each guest to bring along a "special someone."

Kellis intended his Halloween party to serve as the prelude to the upcoming busy season. The unofficial kickoff of that season was actually December 1 when members of the audit staff were expected to begin working 50 hours per week. The weekly workload increased to 55 hours when January 1 arrived. If an engagement fell behind schedule, the audit engagement partner might bump the minimum work week up to 70 hours, or even more, as a deadline approached.

Parties and small talk weren't Bishop's strong suits, but he made it a point to attend each office social function to which he was invited. It was a small price to pay to prevent him from being accurately pegged as a social recluse by his coworkers. Bishop realized that stigma would draw even more attention to him, unwanted attention. He wanted to be as invisible as possible and, ironically, that meant being seen at the office's social events. Of course, at such get-togethers he always took the first reasonable opportunity to slip away after having been seen by all relevant parties.

"Hey, Michael, I mean, 'Harry,' come on in." Michael Bishop was surprised, but it wasn't because Cason Kellis was decked out in an impressive costume intended to represent a cast member from the Broadway musical *Cats*, a skintight costume that included multicolored layers of pancake makeup, a set of six-inch whiskers, and a three-foot tail that curved up behind him and swung to and fro like an upside down pendulum each time that he moved.

Bishop was surprised because Kellis remembered his name. During the meeting earlier that week and the subsequent lunch, Kellis had not once addressed Bishop directly. Bishop was also pleasantly surprised that Kellis recognized that he "was" Harry Potter since his costume didn't do a terrific job of portraying the boy wizard. Then again, anyone faintly familiar with Harry Potter would recognize the lightning bolt scar on his right forehead.

As a child, Bishop had been self-conscious about the scar on the left side of his face. But, as he grew older, he had come to accept that it was a part of who he was. When he was invited to a Halloween party, Bishop typically chose to go as Harry Potter because it meant that he had to add a second scar to his face. It was his way of saying, "Yeah, now I have two scars. So what?"

After a few brief exchanges, Kellis pointed Bishop in the direction of Jim Wilmeth and jokingly suggested that the two of them begin finalizing the audit program for the BRIC engagement.

"Hello, Jim, how are you?" Bishop said as he extended his right hand to Wilmeth who was clutching a whiskey shot glass in his other.

"Doing great, Michael," the already well-lubricated Wilmeth responded.

"I guess being here means that we have made the 'A list' for the office's social circuit."

"No way. Being here simply means that we have been assigned to the chain gang otherwise known as the BRIC audit team," Wilmeth replied as he and Bishop shared a laugh. "Who did you bring to the party? I want to meet the lucky young lady," Wilmeth asked as he looked around in an effort to spot Bishop's date.

"I'm here by myself," Bishop responded quickly and then immediately shifted the focus of the conversation away from him. He chose the most obvious topic for the two of them to discuss, namely, the BRIC Industries audit. "Hey, I was surprised by Suzanne Jennings the other day. She really spoke her mind when it came to her view of auditors."

"No kidding. She is a piece of work, isn't she?" Wilmeth shook his head in disgust. "Can you imagine us getting any audit adjustments past that barracuda? You and Nelson had better not find any major problems during this audit. If we propose any big financial statement adjustments, Jennings will chew Kellis up and spit him out."

Bishop laughed at the thought of the perpetually good-natured Kellis being forced to tell the humorless Jennings that her staff of "expert accountants" had screwed up.

"By the way, have you or Kellis heard anything about the staffing of the BRIC job since our meeting on Monday?" Bishop asked.

After grumbling something to the effect that it wasn't "right to talk shop" at a party, Wilmeth told Bishop that the day before he and Cason Kellis had met with the administrative personnel responsible for making staff assignments to individual engagements. Besides Wilmeth, Lindsay Tankersley would be the only other manager involved in the BRIC audit. Tankersley, a tax manager, would spend several days near the end of the audit making sure that BRIC's deferred tax accounts were in shape.

"Kellis doesn't think that Nelson or you can handle the deferred tax accounts for a large public company—and he and I sure as hell aren't going to spend weeks trying to unravel that b.s."

According to Wilmeth—whose alter ego was Elvis Presley—Jackson Coleman and Becky Linton, staff accountants who had been with the firm for two years, had been assigned to the BRIC job. Both of the staff accountants had worked on previous audits overseen by Kellis. Since each of them had more than two years of experience, Kellis believed that they wouldn't require much supervision, but neither came highly recommended. In fact, Kellis had told Wilmeth that Coleman and Linton would likely be counseled out of the firm once the busy season ended because neither of them was "cut out" to be an audit senior.

In addition to Coleman and Linton, Wilmeth told Bishop that four "rookie" staff accountants would eventually be assigned to the BRIC audit team. Because of their inexperience, the staff accountants would be given relatively simple tasks to perform on the audit.

Besides Nelson and Bishop, two other audit seniors would be working on the BRIC engagement. John Kelly, a computer audit specialist, would be assisting Paula Henderson in performing the internal control tests for the audit. Henderson had previously spent four years on the audit staff of another Big Four firm. For the past three years, she had been a SOX (Sarbanes-Oxley) compliance specialist for a large public company. Wilmeth explained to Bishop that the staffing shortage within their office had gotten to such a critical point that former public accountants, such as Henderson, were being actively recruited.

"We're so desperate for experienced audit staff that pretty soon we will all be trolling the downtown streets wearing help-wanted sandwich boards during our lunch breaks," Wilmeth joked as he tried to get the attention of one of several Hooters girls Kellis had hired to serve as cocktail waitresses for his party.

"So, is Emma going to supervise Paula and John?" Bishop asked.

"Well, here's the deal," Wilmeth began. "Kellis has come up with this bright idea of putting Henderson, Kelly, and the 'floating rookies' that are nabbed to assist them in another office at the client's site."

Wilmeth and Bishop's practice office had recently implemented a new "floating staff" strategy that allowed engagement teams to request additional rookies as needed from a bullpen of newly hired staff accountants. Individual floaters could be requisitioned for a maximum of two weeks for any one audit engagement.

"Henderson will organize and supervise all the internal control testing since that is her area of expertise. Kellis thinks the control tests are a waste of time, so he is going to have Henderson and her squad work independently of the rest of the engagement team." Wilmeth finally flagged down a Hooters girl and ordered another drink before turning back to Bishop. "To answer your question, technically, I will be supervising Henderson and Kelly, but we are hoping that she can pretty much take care of all of the internal control work without much interaction with the main body of the audit team."

"Hmm. That's different," Bishop mused.

"Yeah, different and pretty much off-the-wall stupid, if you ask me," Wilmeth responded derisively. "We will have to make it look like the control work is fully integrated into the audit or we might get zinged if the BRIC audit is looked at by the peer reviewers, or, even worse, by the PCAOB Gestapo."

As an afterthought, Wilmeth told Bishop that BRIC had also committed to loaning internal auditors to the audit team on an as-needed basis. The internal auditors would help with low-level tasks on the audit such as tracking down client documents for internal control tests.

"Kellis is not too happy with the ragtag, last-minute staffing of the BRIC audit," Wilmeth continued. "He asked for a couple more experienced staff accountants in addition to Coleman and Linton but was told that there weren't any available. And he didn't really want to take on Henderson because he thinks it will take her quite awhile to get back up to speed since she has been out of public accounting for a while."

"For a job this large, it seems that we are going to be shorthanded," Bishop commented.

"Well, this is actually a fairly straightforward audit given the nature of the client's business. A lot of the work is tedious, high-volume sort of audit tests that even rookies can do if they are properly supervised. So, we should be able to get by with a bottom-heavy engagement team," Wilmeth explained. "But you're right. Any way you look at it, we are going to be shorthanded. I will be working simultaneously on the audit of that new hospital client. Since I don't have any background in the healthcare industry, that audit is going to suck up a lot of my time even though it is a much smaller engagement than the BRIC job."

Wilmeth paused as his attention was momentarily compromised by the Hooters girl in a Marilyn Monroe wig who had just delivered his next drink.

"Hey, Gorgeous, where have you been all my life?" Wilmeth said suggestively as he placed his arm lightly around the waitress's waist.

"With my husband and two-year-old daughter," the faux blonde replied as she pushed away Wilmeth's arm and headed for her next delivery.

"Wow, she snapped me off," Wilmeth said with a laugh as he turned back to face Michael Bishop. During his previous assignment with Wilmeth, Bishop recalled that the audit manager had been going through a nasty divorce. Given the job-related stress and heavy workload in public accounting, divorce was an all-too frequent occurrence among audit professionals.

"You may not have heard," Wilmeth remarked as he picked up where he had left on in his conversation with Bishop, "but the PCAOB auditors came down really hard on Kellis this past summer for an oil and gas audit that he pretty much butchered last year. He's convinced that he's one of the top candidates to be promoted to OMP when Todd Wilson retires in a few years, and he sure as hell can't afford any more negative attention, especially from the feds."

Bishop was surprised that Wilmeth was sharing such sensitive information with him. Then again, Mr. Jack Daniels, no doubt, was lowering Wilmeth's inhibitions.

"What do you think? Is Kellis a strong candidate for the OMP job?" Bishop asked.

"He probably has a reasonable shot at it. Then again, that's a decision made way above my pay grade and by people who I will never meet. You know, he spent two years in the national office immediately after making partner—that was right after his second divorce," Wilmeth whispered discreetly before adding, "Katy, the Dallas Cowboy cheerleader over there by the bar, is round three."

Wilmeth took a sip of his drink to give Bishop a chance to pick Kellis's present wife out of a group of costumed party animals clustered around a large mahogany bar.

"Anyway, I'm sure he made some good connections up there with several of the executive partners. He followed that up by doing a three-year rotation in Europe with the firm's Brussels, Luxembourg, and London offices. That's the kind of background that is a good prep for a high profile position like the OMP for our office, which, of course, is one of the largest in the firm. But I think he actually has his sights set even higher."

"You mean like managing partner of the firm?"

"Oh yeah. There's no limit to that little whippersnapper's ambition," Wilmeth replied with a sneer. "You know, he's not even forty yet, so he has the time to build a resume for the top job."

Bishop decided to ask a question for which he knew the answer just to see how Wilmeth would respond.

"So, I guess he asked to be assigned to the BRIC engagement since it is one of the largest in the office?"

Wilmeth laughed aloud at Bishop's question. "No way, Mikey. Just the opposite was true. That little prima donna went postal when Todd Wilson told him that he would be heading up the BRIC audit. Wilson probably thought that taking on a crappy assignment like the BRIC engagement would be good for Kellis after he screwed up that oil and gas audit last year. A little comeuppance for him, you know. Kellis has been all high and mighty since Wilson came up with the idea to create that biotech group within the office and put him in charge of it."

Wilmeth's multiple references to the botched oil and gas audit overseen by Kellis made Bishop curious regarding what had happened on that engagement. But he didn't think it was appropriate to ask Wilmeth to explain those comments, and he didn't want to come across as a busybody.

After finishing off his latest drink, Wilmeth continued. "Hey, don't get me wrong. I actually like Kellis. Even though he is a conniving, pompous, underhanded little social climber, he knows how to have fun, if you know what I mean," Wilmeth added with a sideways wink at Bishop.

Bishop wasn't sure exactly what the latter comment meant either. He had heard that Kellis enjoyed partying and that sometimes he was less than discreet—but surely he wasn't as indiscreet as Wilmeth, Bishop thought to himself.

Wilmeth put his hand on Bishop's shoulder as he leaned forward to speak more privately. "Michael, I can get away with saying things like that because I'm on the ten-year plan."

"Ten-year plan? I'm not sure what you mean?"

Wilmeth leaned in even further before he spoke again, so close that Bishop thought he might get a buzz from inhaling second-hand whiskey vapors. "Everyone knows, me included, that after I have put in ten years with the firm, I'll be shown the door. No way in hell am I going to make partner. So, I can afford to speak my mind unlike those fast-track managers who are trying to brownnose their way to becoming partner."

Bishop wasn't sure how to react to Wilmeth's true confessions so he simply smiled and nodded his head.

After suggesting that he needed to do some "mingling," Wilmeth surprised Bishop with his parting comment. "You know, Michael, I have a pretty good idea that you will sign up on the ten-year plan yourself eventually, if you haven't already. I think you're a lot like me. You're smarter and more competent than those audit seniors who kowtow and suck up to the partners, but you're not willing to sell out to get to the top." With that, Wilmeth slapped Bishop lightly on the back and walked away.

For the next few minutes, Bishop sipped on a 7-Up that he had picked up at the bar as he drifted aimlessly looking for another familiar face in the large crowd.

Although he was a teetotaler, Bishop wasn't self-righteous when it came to drinking. He simply didn't like his senses dulled by any foreign substance.

"Hey, Michael, come over here."

Bishop turned to find Emma Nelson standing several feet away decked out in an ostentatious, floor-length Mother Goose costume that included a powdered wig and a huge pointed hat.

"Michael, I want you to meet Jackson Coleman and Becky Linton," Nelson said as she motioned to the two individuals to her immediate right. "They will be working with us on the BRIC audit."

"In fact, Jim Wilmeth, I mean, Elvis over there," Bishop said as he pointed out Jim Wilmeth on the other side of the room, "just told me that the two of you would be working with us."

Bishop extended his right hand first to Linton, a petite redhead with a milky complexion dotted with freckles who was outfitted in Pilgrim garb, and then to Coleman who was not only dressed like the TV sitcom character Sheldon Cooper—he was wearing a Green Lantern t-shirt and a pair of tight-legged pants—but was a dead ringer for him as well.

"I guess he also told you that Paula Henderson would be working on the BRIC job," Nelson said.

"Yes, he did. Do you know if she is here?" Bishop asked as if he was interested in meeting Henderson, which he wasn't.

"I was told she has a couple of small children, so I'm guessing she won't make it," Nelson responded. "It would probably be a real challenge for her to make it out on a weeknight."

An awkward lull in the conversation prompted Bishop to address Coleman.

"Well, Jackson, are you ready for another busy season?"

"Bazinga, am I ever. I just can't wait to get my hands on all of those numbers," Coleman responded energetically, staying in character.

Bishop then turned to Becky.

"What about you Becky? Are you looking forward to turning BRIC Industries' accounting records inside out?"

The apparently painfully shy redhead smiled demurely and then pivoted her head at an angle before slowly nodding it diagonally, signaling who knew what.

Bishop waited for several moments before he spoke again because he assumed that Becky would eventually say something, anything. When it became apparent that verbal skills were not one of Becky's strong suits, Bishop glanced at Nelson who was also waiting for her new subordinate to verbalize. Finally, Bishop nodded his head ambiguously at Becky and then turned and complimented Nelson on her costume.

"Well, thank you, Michael," Emma said as she subtly peeked over his shoulder looking for someone who would give her an excuse to excuse herself.

The four of them stood there silently for an eternity lasting 30 seconds, each hoping that one of the other three would pick up the conversation ball and run with it. Fortunately, an interloper rescued them.

"Hello, are you Michael Bishop?" the stranger a/k/a the Lone Ranger asked.

"Yes. That's me," Bishop replied to the masked man.

"Oh, John, I'm glad you're here," Nelson interjected. "I guess you haven't met Michael yet. Michael, this is John Kelly. He is the computer audit specialist who will be working with us on the BRIC audit."

As Bishop and Kelly shook hands, Nelson added, "Well, actually, John, you will be spending your time on the audit working with Paula. Isn't that right?"

"Yep, that's what I was told by Jim Wilmeth."

Kelly and Nelson stood side by side as they faced Bishop. Immediately, Bishop sensed that something was up. The two of them were standing a little too close to each other, invading each other's private space. And, when they looked at each other, their eyes were sending coded messages. Bishop's sixth sense was seldom wrong and it was telling him loud and clear that the Lone Ranger and Mother Goose were an item.

Bishop forced himself to stand there for the next ten minutes or so and engage in the smallest of small talk, some of which was so tiny that it just involved head nodding. When he decided that he had filled his quota for face time with his four coworkers, he excused himself.

For the next 45 minutes, Bishop spoke briefly with an assortment of cowboys and Native Americans, construction workers, bikers, and police officers. Finally, when he confirmed that Cason Kellis's back was turned, he slipped out an unlocked side door that led to a patio that provided a clear path to the cul-de-sac where he had parked his car.

As soon as Bishop stepped onto the patio, he bumped into a couple sharing a vigorous kiss. When the Lone Ranger loosened his lip-lock on Mother Goose, Bishop found himself staring straight into Emma Nelson's eyes which immediately grew to the size of miniature radar dishes. Bishop quickly excused himself and slipped by the twosome and continued on his way to his car.

As he was driving home, Bishop realized that he had been assigned to possibly the most dysfunctional audit engagement team that had ever been assembled. Despite the challenges that the beyond odd mix of personalities would pose, he was actually looking forward to busy season. The long workdays of winter would serve to keep his mind off other issues.

Chapter 4

Friday, November 15

"Okay, are you guys ready to get started?" Cason Kellis asked as he clapped his hands enthusiastically. "We need to get this show on the road."

Cason Kellis, Jim Wilmeth, Emma Nelson, and Michael Bishop were meeting in a cozy conference room of their practice office. The meeting would serve as the annual fraud brainstorming session for the BRIC Industries audit. The professional standards mandated that such a session be held for every audit but only "key members" of an audit engagement team were required to be present, which meant that staff accountants were generally excluded. Michael Bishop had been looking forward to the meeting, which would be his first. He was curious whether the fraud discussions were perfunctory bull sessions intended to satisfy the explicit requirement for them in the professional standards or whether they were meaningful efforts to identify potential fraud in a client's financial statements and underlying accounting records.

Bishop realized that until the late 1980s professional auditing standards had never explicitly referred to the term "fraud." For decades, rule-making authorities within the U.S. auditing profession had refused to incorporate that term in the auditing standards, presumably to mitigate auditors' legal exposure when they failed to discover fraud. In Bishop's mind, that had been an indefensible position since he believed that the primary role of independent auditors was to search for intentional misrepresentations in clients' financial statements.

Neither Paula Henderson nor John Kelly was present at the meeting—Henderson was away from the office attending a training session, while Kelly's absence was never addressed. Privately, Bishop was disappointed that Kelly wasn't there because it would have been entertaining to observe Nelson and Kelly as they tried to avoid making goo-goo eyes at each other. Although, the firm didn't expressly forbid intra-office dating, it was definitely frowned upon. Even the firm's young professionals generally considered intra-office dating tacky, if not adolescent.

Since observing Nelson and Kelly kissing at Kellis's party, Bishop had spoken with her on a couple of occasions but had not referred to the incident. On each occasion, Nelson had been uncomfortable, no doubt because she was concerned that Bishop might mention their embarrassing run-in. Although he found it entertaining to watch Nelson squirm uncomfortably each time they met, Bishop had no intention of mentioning the incident to her or to anyone else, for that matter.

"I've asked Emma to lead the discussion today since she is the old hand on the BRIC engagement," Kellis said as he took the seat to Nelson's immediate left at the small, circular conference room table. Kellis then reached over and softly squeezed Nelson's left forearm to relieve any tension she might have or to signal her to begin the session or to simply take an opportunity to paw her in public.

"Well, thank you very much … Cason. This will be my first time to lead one of these sessions so please excuse me if I appear a little nervous."

"Emma, come on. You're my main girl. You're going to do just fine," Kellis reassured Nelson.

"I have asked Michael to be the note taker for this meeting," Nelson began as she glanced down at a stapled document of 20 or more pages that she had laid in front of her. "In the next day or so, I will email each of you his electronic file of notes after I have had a chance to review and update them."

Bishop, who was poised in front of his laptop across the table from Nelson, expected his mediocre typing skills to be tested over the next couple of hours.

"Our primary objective today is to quote-unquote 'brainstorm' regarding how BRIC Industries' accounting records and financial statements might be susceptible to fraud. As we all know, that requirement is included in the auditing standards," Nelson said as she glanced at her notes. "Plus, we are supposed to consider how BRIC's management might perpetrate and conceal such fraud and address some other issues such as identifying specific fraud risk factors for this engagement."

Nelson looked up from her notes as she addressed Kellis.

"I hope you understand … Cason … that I know … that we all know, that there is practically no chance that we will discover any fraud during this audit. With someone like Suzanne Jennings in charge of the accounting and financial reporting and … and, uh, related stuff for this company, there is no way, well, almost no way that any fraud could happen."

"Yeah, you are right about that, Emma." Kellis reached over and patted Nelson on her shoulder. "There's not much chance of anything fishy going on in this company's accounting department while Field Marshal Jennings is in charge," he added with a chuckle.

"Thank you … Cason," Nelson said as she smiled broadly at Kellis. "I'm glad that we agree on that."

Jim Wilmeth rolled his eyes in a show of disbelief or disgust as he glanced at Bishop. Bishop wasn't sure whether Wilmeth was signaling that he disagreed with the initial fraud assessment shared by Nelson and Kellis or that he was disgusted by the lovefest that was playing out in front of him.

"Okay, with that out of the way," Nelson continued, "I want to begin by reviewing the fraud triangle. The fraud triangle has three angles. Those three angles are incentives slash pressures, opportunities, and attitudes slash rationalizations. Let's begin with incentives slash pressures. This angle of the fraud triangle refers to factors or circumstances that increase the likelihood that client management will engage in some type of fraudulent conduct. That likelihood is increased when such factors are present. These factors include such factors as a significant ownership in the entity to be audited by senior management ..."

As Nelson read word-for-word from the stapled document, her three colleagues soon realized that document was a typewritten script for her presentation, a verbose and poorly edited script that she must have spent hours developing.

While Nelson kept her eyes trained on her script, Wilmeth intercepted Kellis's gaze and then silently mouthed the words, "What the hell is she doing?"

Kellis grimaced and shook his head ever so slightly.

"Now, let's review the second angle of the fraud triangle. Opportunities refer to — "

"Uh, just a minute," Kellis interjected, cutting off Nelson in mid-sentence. "Emma, we appreciate your taking the time to update us on the finer points of the fraud triangle, but I think that we should probably cut to the chase and begin discussing specific fraud issues for BRIC Industries."

Kellis's statement threw a monkey wrench into Nelson's grand plan for the meeting. For a few moments she looked at him unsure exactly how to proceed. Then, she began anxiously flipping through her script trying to find a new starting point.

"Uh, okay. So, let's see," Nelson said as she turned to the fourth or fifth page of her notes. "Maybe I should review the standard types of fraud risk factors that are identified in the auditing standards."

"Emma, I really don't think that is necessary either," Kellis stated decisively. "Not that reviewing that material is unimportant, but today we are kind of rushed for time. So, again, maybe we should just focus on the fraud issues specifically relevant to BRIC."

Now totally flustered, Nelson blurted out, "I'm sorry, but I was just going to highlight what the auditing standards require when it comes to searching for fraud since there isn't much to say regarding the likelihood of fraud happening with this client. Like I said, I've never led this type of discussion before." In the span of a few moments, Nelson went from flustered to flummoxed to tearful. "I guess that it was my responsibility to ask you exactly what you expected me to discuss at this meeting."

"Emmie, Emmie, you're fine. I understand completely and, again, I totally agree with you that when it comes to fraud, there isn't much to say with respect to this client." After reassuring Nelson with a firm squeeze of her forearm, Kellis added, "What is probably most efficient is for us to first review the summary audit memorandum for last year's audit and see what issues were identified in that document. Then, we can scan the audited financial statements from last year and the year-to-date financial statements for the first three quarters of the current year. After that, we can review press releases issued by the company and other reports in the media that identify recent developments within BRIC's industry and the overall economy that might be relevant to our discussion."

A demoralized Nelson stared blankly at Kellis after he outlined his impromptu agenda for the meeting.

"Do you have those items?" Kellis asked.

"Uh, well, uh … not all of them," Nelson replied timidly.

"I tell you what, Emmie. You and I are going back to my office and put our heads together and organize everything that we need for this meeting. It's about time that I got 'hands on' for this engagement anyway." Kellis paused as he turned to Wilmeth, "Jim, why don't you and Michael meet us back here in an hour. Once Emma and I get everything organized, I think it will only take us ninety minutes or so to wrap this up."

———————

Wilmeth invited Bishop to come to his office while Kellis helped the visibly shaken Nelson recover from her abortive attempt to lead the brainstorming session.

After they were safely out of earshot of their two colleagues, Wilmeth turned to Bishop. "That's what happens when you give someone a big assignment but don't give her any instructions or supervision."

Bishop didn't respond. He didn't want to openly criticize Nelson or Kellis.

"You know, she's only supervised the fieldwork on a couple of small audits. The brainstorming sessions on those jobs may have taken thirty minutes to complete, if that. Last year, she was a senior on this audit, but she didn't supervise the fieldwork. I'm guessing that she didn't sit in on the fraud planning session since she was basically a glorified staff accountant at the time."

"Kind of like me this year," Bishop said with a chuckle.

"Come on, Michael. I'm guessing that it doesn't bother you in the least that you're shadowing Emmie on this job. If the truth is known, you're probably happy that she's in charge. And you're going to be really happy if this thing blows up since it won't be your fault."

"Do you think there is any chance of that?" Bishop asked.

"Oh, I just know Kellis. He is really ticked off that he was assigned to this job." Wilmeth leaned forward and lowered his voice as they walked down the long corridor that led to his office. "This is on the down low, okay? Kellis is coming very close to landing those two big biotech clients that he has been recruiting for the past six months. If he can corral those two companies, then he will be taken off the BRIC engagement as soon as this audit is wrapped up. So, there is no reason for him to invest much time or effort in the audit. I guarantee you that all he wants to do is get it behind him as quickly and quietly as possible. That sort of attitude on the part of the audit engagement partner is the prime ingredient for a blown audit."

Wilmeth closed the door of his office behind Bishop. After the two sat down, Wilmeth continued. "But, the point is, he had better be careful because he can't afford another blotch on his record. That night at his Halloween party I mentioned the audit of his oil and gas client that caused the office, and the firm, to catch a lot of flak from the PCAOB."

"Yeah, you did briefly mention that," Bishop confirmed.

"I wouldn't tell most audit seniors this, but let's just say that he may have gotten caught making a few changes in some work papers after they had been archived. When he found out that the audit had been selected for review by the PCAOB inspection team coming to our office, he went in and cleaned up some issues that had been left hanging in the work papers. From what I heard, Kellis had allowed the client to get away with understating its bad debt reserve and front-loading revenue on some big take-or-pay contracts. He altered the work papers to make those decisions appear to be justified when, in fact, they weren't."

"Wow, that's pretty serious stuff," Bishop said without thinking.

"Yeah, that's an understatement. Mind you now, there was another rumor floating around that rather than making the work paper changes himself, Kellis ordered an audit senior to make them. But whoever it was didn't document any of the changes. They also tried to cover their tracks by changing the electronic time stamp on the work papers. Despite that, the PCAOB inspectors discovered the changes. The PCAOB could have thrown the book at him, but for some reason they let him off the hook. Maybe the changes that were made weren't that serious. Or, maybe, they couldn't prove who had actually made the changes. Who knows? But, the point is, the guy is just damn reckless at times."

"You would think that after you've been through something like that, you would be inclined to toe the line," Bishop suggested.

"No way. You don't know Kellis like I know Kellis. The more the guy gets away with, the more he thinks he can get away with," Wilmeth responded. "Plus, he has brought in so much business for the office and the firm that he feels he is insulated from any bad decisions that he makes."

Wilmeth glanced at a message on his iPad before continuing.

"Bottom line, you have to give him credit. He may not be much of an auditor, but he has a helluva lot of self-confidence and the perseverance of a pit bull. Once he sets a goal for himself, he goes after it with a vengeance. That's why I wouldn't be shocked if he becomes the next OMP. I think his primary motivation is to prove something to his old man who is a retired federal judge. After a few drinks one night, Kellis told me that his father never thought he would make anything of himself."

Bishop was once more surprised that Wilmeth was sharing so much office scuttlebutt with him—on this occasion, there was no Jack Daniels to blame. The suggestion that Kellis had been responsible for undocumented changes in work papers after the given audit had been completed was startling to Bishop. And Bishop's head was still spinning from what he had heard a few minutes earlier. He couldn't believe that Kellis had reinforced Nelson's opinion that the likelihood of fraud in BRIC's accounting records and financial statements was next to nil. To the contrary, Bishop saw red flags everywhere suggesting that the risk of fraud was much higher than normal for this client.

"By the way, Jim, I was curious about what you thought of Kellis's statement regarding the likelihood of fraud affecting BRIC's financial statements. You know, when Emma said there was basically no chance that BRIC's financial statements could be impacted by fraud given that Suzanne Jennings is in charge?"

Bishop didn't normally ask such probing questions of his superiors, but there was time to kill and Wilmeth seemed more than willing to provide his opinions on even the most sensitive topics.

"Yeah, that was definitely wacky. The fact that Jennings is in charge doesn't lower the risk of fraud, it increases it—by a factor of ten. Kellis and I have had a couple of meetings with her since that first meeting you were in a few weeks ago. There is no doubt that she has a warped view of financial reporting. She sees financial reporting as a way to help accomplish the company's goals rather than to provide full and fair disclosure to investors." Wilmeth propped his feet on the top of his desk and then yawned. "But that doesn't have much impact on us. We're going to go in there and tick and tie and make the audit work papers look good and wind up issuing a clean opinion like we always do." Wilmeth paused before adding, "And then, we are going to cross our fingers and hope like hell that BRIC is guilty of no more than 'fine tuning' its financial statements rather than engaging in a full-scale fraud."

"I was wondering whether that rumored buyout of BRIC by a private equity fund might cause the company's executives to be even more inclined to, uh, 'fine tune,' as you say, BRIC's financial statements," Bishop asked.

"Oh yeah, sure it will. All the accruals will be tight as a new pair of shoes and they are going to stretch the sales cutoff as much as possible and you can bet that they will defer or capitalize any expenses that they can. They will want to do everything possible to put the company in the best possible light. Plus, they are going to make damn sure that BRIC reaches or surpasses the consensus earnings estimate put out for the fourth quarter by the Wall Street securities analysts who track the company."

Once more, Bishop was shocked by Wilmeth's candor.

"I spoke to Cody DeBurger, the audit manager who was on the job the past three years," Wilmeth continued. "He said that the company is always cheating around the edges, including understating the year-end accruals for the soft numbers such as the warranty reserve and even some of the hard numbers like accrued wages and salaries. He told me, in particular, that the bad debt allowance is always significantly understated. He said that over the past few years BRIC has become the supplier of last resort, meaning that it extends credit to high-risk customers that its competitors turn away. That has led to a collection problem that the company conveniently ignores when its calculating the year-end allowance."

After answering a phone call, Wilmeth picked up where he had left off. "BRIC missed its consensus earnings estimate by two cents for the third quarter when Jennings was over in Europe with Hakes and Zimmer, the CEO and COO, trying to drum up business for the company. DeBurger said that she is obsessed with making sure that the quarterly earnings per share number doesn't fall short of the consensus earnings estimate put out by Wall Street."

"Despite that, didn't the company continue its string of consecutive quarters in which it has reported increases in sales?"

"Yeah, somehow they managed to keep that winning streak intact ... barely," Wilmeth replied cynically. "That trend is sacred to Jennings. But I guarantee you that come hell or high water she is not going to let BRIC come up short of its consensus earnings estimate again. That two-cent miss doesn't sound like much, but it caused the company's stock to be pummeled in the market. The stock price was down twelve to fifteen percent within a few days. There's no doubt that's why the company's P.R. department issued three press releases in the past few weeks to try to get the stock price back up."

"What was in the press releases?"

"Oh, Hakes and Zimmer announced that BRIC has a couple of business ventures in the works and that they have a plan to reduce production costs significantly in three of the company's four divisions. And they supposedly are negotiating some big contract with a government agency. Stuff like that," Wilmeth responded. "Who knows if any of that is true, but the stock price has recovered quite a bit since those announcements were made. Of course, the rumors circulating about that private equity fund buying out BRIC has also helped prop up the stock price."

"So, none of those things are going to affect our audit?"

"Nah, not really," Wilmeth replied as he slowly shook his head from side to side. "Like I said, we are going in there and do all the audit procedures, propose a few audit adjustments, and then roll over and sign off on whatever earnings per share number the company comes up with. Kellis is not one of those confrontational guys. He's in to 'client service.' You know, keep 'em happy and don't give 'em any reason to even think about switching to another audit firm. Plus, like I said, he just wants to get this audit done as quickly as possible so that he can move on to bigger and better things."

As Bishop sat there soaking up everything being said by Wilmeth, every preconception he had of independent auditing, audit partners, corporate executives, and financial reporting, in general, was being confirmed.

"Now, Michael," Wilmeth said as he leaned forward and propped his elbows on his desk. "You're smart enough to know that you can't repeat any of what I've just said outside of this office. I'm a short-timer here, and I'm only sharing this with you because I think you and I are on the same wavelength."

"Sure, Jim. I understand."

"Besides," Wilmeth quickly added with a laugh, "it may just be that this is all sour grapes on my part. If I had a chance in hell of making partner, I might be rolling over and selling my soul just like all those slick, smooth-talking country club types that make up the new partner class every year."

———

When Wilmeth and Bishop returned to the small conference room, Kellis and Nelson were putting the finishing touches on some PowerPoint slides. Shortly after Nelson began walking through the slides, Bishop realized that they were altered—superficially altered—versions of a series of slides that had been used in the one-week training session that he had attended for newly-promoted audit seniors. During the given in-class exercise, Bishop and his peers were organized into three-person audit teams that were required to carry out a fraud brainstorming session for a hypothetical and generic manufacturing company, a company not dissimilar to BRIC Industries. Each group was provided with a company history, extensive financial data for the company, and other relevant information, such as key industry norms. The participants were required to identify financial statement items at risk of being intentionally misstated, specific methods that the company's management might use to perpetrate and conceal intentional misrepresentations, and fraud risk factors that were relevant to the hypothetical client. At the conclusion of the exercise, the audit seniors had been provided with the "official solution" that consisted of the slides that Kellis and Nelson had doctored to make them apply as closely as possible to the upcoming BRIC audit.

Not surprisingly, the at-risk financial statement items identified by Kellis and Nelson were the usual suspects in a financial statement fraud. Those items included the allowances for bad debts and inventory obsolescence, the warranty reserve, the reserve for sales returns, each of the major year-end expense accruals, and, as always, suspect No. 1, sales. After identifying those items, Kellis and Nelson took turns explaining how management might misrepresent each of them.

For the allowance for bad debts, Nelson provided the grossly unimaginative suggestion that "management might intentionally understate the year-end allowance for bad debts." The explanations provided by Kellis were more eloquent but not much more informative.

The final topic addressed by Kellis and Nelson were potential fraud risk factors that were relevant to BRIC's operations or its management team. At this point, Nelson apparently veered from the agenda that she and Kellis had prepared. No doubt, she did so to try to impress Kellis with her knowledge of the relevant auditing standards.

Nelson began by indicating that while preparing for the brainstorming session she had reviewed the list of fraud risk factors included in an appendix of the auditing standards. "I did find that several of those factors were potentially relevant to the BRIC audit. For example, top management has been granted a large number of stock options as a part of their compensation package. I have also heard that management is very proud of the fact that the company has reported increases in revenues for the past so many quarters. That might give management an incentive to — "

"Emma," Kellis interrupted Nelson. "I see where you're going, but I'm not sure that it's necessary in this case. We have already established that this is a very reputable management team with an unmatched record of integrity."

Despite the emphasis that Kellis placed on the terms "reputable" and "unmatched," Bishop was certain that the audit partner didn't believe a word that he had just spoken.

"Uh, okay. I understand," Nelson replied contritely. "And just to, uh, repeat what I said earlier, I believe that, given the leadership of Suzanne Jennings, we don't have anything to worry about when it comes to fraud. But I thought that we should go ahead and at least list the fraud risk factors that are even remotely relevant to this audit."

"Again, Emma," Kellis began as he reached over and stroked her left arm. "We appreciate your research and the fact that you are so on top of the specific requirements that are buried deep in the bowels of the auditing standards. But you have to remember that it is our professional judgment as auditors that should dictate what we do during the course of any given engagement, including in the planning stage, which is where we are now. And, in my informed opinion, I don't think it is necessary to develop a comprehensive laundry list that includes potential fraud risk factors that are no more than remotely relevant to this client."

When Kellis paused to give Nelson an opportunity to speak, her only response was a barely audible, "Okay."

After commenting on a few other matters, the brainstorming session effectively ended after only 45 minutes. Rather than a brainstorming session, the meeting had been more of a tag team lecture by Kellis and Nelson since neither Wilmeth nor Bishop were asked to provide any input. Despite Kellis's earlier comments, no references were made to the prior year's summary audit memorandum or to any BRIC press releases or other media reports relevant to the company or its industry.

"Well, see there, Emma. That wasn't painful at all, was it?" Kellis said playfully to Nelson.

"No, it wasn't," Nelson replied. "I really appreciate your help … Cason. There's probably not many audit partners who would take time out from their busy schedules to help me like you did."

"Any time, Sweetheart," Kellis responded.

Bishop didn't glance at Wilmeth to take in his reaction to the gushy dialogue, but he could almost hear Wilmeth's skin crawling.

"Okay, I will make sure that these slides get saved to the electronic planning files for this year's audit," Nelson said. After a brief pause, Nelson spoke again, this time with a quizzical look on her face. "To be honest, I have only been involved in two of these sessions before today. Near the end of each one of them, we talked about how the audit program from the prior year should be changed as a result of the fraud risk issues we discussed and whether any changes should be made in the audit budget from the previous year." Nelson turned to face Kellis who was preparing to leave because he thought that the meeting had already ended. "Like, uh, should we make some changes in the audit procedures for the financial statement items that we discussed? And, uh, should we increase the audit budget for one or more of those items?"

Nelson's questions made Bishop once again suspect that she was trying to earn points with Kellis by demonstrating her understanding of the audit planning process. Then again, maybe she was simply doing her job as the supervising audit senior by raising a couple of relevant and important questions.

When Kellis didn't respond immediately to the questions posed by Nelson, she spoke again. "For example, since we identified the bad debt allowance as an at-risk financial statement item, should we increase the audit budget for that account?"

Kellis leaned back in his chair for several moments as he tried to convey that he was deep in thought.

"Well, you know, Emma, we will be applying a rubber yardstick to every one of those reserve and allowance accounts and the discretionary year-end accruals. And that is true on every audit for those types of accounts. So, no, I don't think we need to adjust the audit budget." Kellis paused momentarily. It was obvious to both Wilmeth and Bishop that he was simply "blowing smoke" to confuse Nelson and hopefully cause her to stop asking meaningful questions. "In terms of specific audit procedures that we will apply and the types of audit evidence that we are going to collect, I think that we should basically invoke the SALY concept."

" 'Sally?' Uh, I'm sorry but I don't understand," Nelson confessed.

"Same … as … last … year." Kellis spoke the words slowly and distinctively for Nelson's benefit.

"Oh … I see," a baffled Nelson responded.

"You know, there is one change that I would suggest," Kellis added as he closed his briefcase. "Since there has been absolutely no indication of any fraud on the part of this client over the twenty-five or so years that our firm has audited the company, I think we can rely on a higher proportion of 'soft evidence' than normal this year. By 'soft,' I mean such evidence as the results of analytical tests. For example, we might use a disproportionate number of reasonableness tests to vouch revenue and expense items."

For the first time during the meeting, Kellis asked for the input of his primary subordinate on the engagement. "Jim, what do you think? You think that's a reasonable strategy? At a minimum, I know that would speed up the audit."

"Oh yeah. I'm in total agreement with you," Wilmeth responded forcefully. "We know that Suzanne Jennings is not going to put up with any b.s. So, sure, I think we are fine in relying on some of the softer forms of evidence. In fact, sending only negative receivable confirmations to the client's customers would save lots of time since we wouldn't have to track down all of the exceptions that are reported when we send out positives."

The fact that Wilmeth had completely contradicted what he had said a short while earlier in his office regarding Jennings' likely impact on BRIC's fraud risk did not escape Bishop's attention. Also catching his attention was a subtle change in the tone of Wilmeth's voice when he made the statement regarding the exclusive use of negative confirmations for BRIC's receivables. Bishop detected an underlying sarcasm to that tone, sarcasm that may have been too subtle for Kellis to discern.

"Hmm. Hadn't considered that possibility," Kellis responded. "Can we do that?" he asked in all seriousness, which confirmed that he had not detected the cynicism underlying Wilmeth's previous statement.

"Well, I tell you what. I'll research that and get back to you." This time, Wilmeth's response was laced with thinly veiled contempt.

Kellis paused while he studied Wilmeth's face.

"Uh, okay. You do that," the audit partner said tersely.

The tone of Kellis's brief response and the fact that his ears were turning a shade of crimson indicated that he had picked up on the disrespect underlying Wilmeth's previous response.

"While I'm at it, maybe I will go back and see how many of last year's work papers we can just copy and use for the current year," Wilmeth suggested. "That would save even more time."

Bishop was shocked that Wilmeth was trying to anger Kellis.

After a protracted and awkward silence, Kellis finally spoke. "I want to let each of you know where I stand when it comes to this audit," Kellis said slowly and emphatically. For the first time in Bishop's presence, the typically mild-mannered and upbeat partner was neither. "I want all of you and your subordinates to make sure that a softer, gentler approach is used with this client." When Kellis spoke the word "you" he was looking directly at Wilmeth. "For example, there is no need to pester the client by proposing a lot of penny nickel audit adjustments. Avoid stepping on toes and making the client employees and executives angry for no good reason. I don't like the fact that they believe that independent auditors are the enemy. I want you to demonstrate that we are working with them not against them."

As Kellis prattled on, Bishop wondered to himself if the phrase "professional skepticism" meant anything to the accommodating audit partner.

"This is an important point," Kellis continued. "In a private meeting that I had with Suzanne Jennings, she made it crystal clear to me that we dang well better not do anything that would cause BRIC to delay the press release in which she will announce the company's fourth-quarter earnings and the operating results for the fiscal year. The press release is typically issued several days before the company files its 10-K with the SEC."

As Kellis spoke, Wilmeth was ignoring the angry audit partner, concentrating instead on the doodling he was doing on the legal pad in front of him.

"I also want each of you and the staff accountants that you supervise to be well aware of my fifty-fifty rule. I want audit team members to spend fifty percent of their time performing whatever procedure they have been assigned and the other fifty percent documenting that procedure and the results." Kellis paused briefly to underline the importance of his next statement. "I want the work papers to be picture perfect just in case this audit is selected for a peer review or someone else happens to review the work papers."

Bishop was well aware that the "someone else" referred to by Kellis was the PCAOB.

"Finally, I want to make sure that the audit goes smoothly. I don't want any of us to be at odds with each other. Okay?"

When Kellis finished speaking, Wilmeth finally looked up from his legal pad and made eye contact with the audit partner. Wilmeth didn't reply verbally or nonverbally to Kellis's lecture, but it was obvious to Bishop that Kellis's intended reprimand had no impact on the audit manager.

Because she hadn't spoken in a few minutes, Nelson apparently thought she had to say something. "Cason, I just want to add to what you said about the audit adjustments. For some reason, every year that I have been on this audit it seems that the client has gotten more and more upset with the audit adjustments that we propose."

Nelson paused because Kellis was still staring at Wilmeth.

"Oh, go ahead, Emma," Kellis said after glancing at Nelson before turning his attention back to Wilmeth.

"Well, I just wanted to say that you are absolutely correct. I think we should be very careful when we decide to propose audit adjustments. There is no reason to upset the client with a lot of proposed adjustments since we usually decide to pass on the great majority of them anyway."

"Well, thank you, Emma. I'm glad to see that at least you and I are on the same page," Kellis responded while he continued to glare at Wilmeth.

Once more, the thought occurred to Bishop that he was now a member of one of the most dysfunctional audit teams ever assembled.

Chapter 5

Monday, December 2

By the first week of December, Michael Bishop and Emma Nelson had officially moved full time into their "busy season" office on the ninth floor of the ten-story building that served as the corporate headquarters for BRIC Industries. The building was in the midtown business district of the large Midwestern city where their practice office was located. The client's location was perfect for Bishop since it was only three miles from his apartment complex in a nearby suburb.

The suite of offices occupied by Suzanne Jennings and BRIC's other senior executives was on the plush tenth floor of the headquarters building. That floor resembled a high-end art gallery because of the beautiful alabaster statuary and French impressionist art that lined its hallways and walls. Shortly after she arrived at BRIC, Jennings had authorized expenditures of more than $1 million to add an opulent, if not royal, flair to the tenth floor.

The offices of the accounting and finance junior executives, including that of Bud Wallace, the general accounting manager, and the four divisional controllers, were located on the ninth floor. Down a hallway from Wallace's office was the comfortable, spacious, and beautifully decorated conference room that would serve as the workspace for Bishop, Nelson, Jim Wilmeth, and Cason Kellis on the few occasions he would be at the client's headquarters.

Jackson Coleman, Becky Linton, and the rookie staff accountants assigned to the BRIC audit team occupied a corner storage room on the ninth floor that had been converted into a workspace by the addition of several office cubicles. Paula Henderson, John Kelly, and the "floaters" working for them were stashed in another storage room on the building's third floor. That cramped, windowless, and poorly ventilated room was used as a dumping ground for obsolete computers and computer peripherals. The client had cleared enough space in the room for two tables to accommodate the auditors.

Monday, December 2, was technically the first day of busy season since that was the date that the audit staff members of Bishop's employer were supposed to ratchet their work weeks up to 50 hours. Because of the late start on the BRIC internal control tests, which was due to a series of training sessions that Paula Henderson had been required to attend, those tests were several weeks behind schedule. The internal control tests were typically begun in October and were nearing completion by the end of December. So, when the first week of December rolled around, Henderson and her crew were already working 60-hour weeks.

―――――――

Since the brainstorming session two weeks earlier, Bishop and Nelson had spent most of their time at BRIC working on administrative and planning tasks for the audit. Nelson had appointed Bishop as the timekeeper for the engagement, made him responsible for the correspondence file, and asked him to update the permanent work paper files with the help of Jackson Coleman and Becky Linton.

Bishop would be filing weekly time reports each Friday with Nelson. She would review those reports and then pass them on to Wilmeth and Kellis. She asked Bishop to redesign the time report format used on the previous year's audit to make it more informative. She wanted the weekly reports to flag any audit tasks that were falling significantly behind schedule. Nelson also asked Bishop to develop a series of Gantt charts to make it easier for her, Wilmeth, and Kellis to gauge the progress being made on the audit.

Nelson instructed Bishop to review the correspondence file and update it for changes that had occurred over the previous year. To ensure as high a return rate as possible for receivables, payables, and bank confirmations, the audit team needed to have reliable contact information for BRIC's customers, suppliers, and banks. The audit team also needed reliable contact information for BRIC's external law firms, regulatory agencies with which the company frequently interacted, and a number of other entities.

The permanent files for the BRIC engagement included documents such as the company's articles of incorporation, corporate charter, bylaws, bond indentures and other major contracts, the chart of accounts, organizational charts for each department, and several audit checklists. Each of those documents had to be reviewed and, if necessary, updated, to ensure that the auditors were aware of any major changes in BRIC's operations over the previous twelve months and to determine what, if any, audit implications those changes had.

Also included in the permanent work paper files was a large Excel spreadsheet that contained a quarter-by-quarter analysis of the current ratio, the inventory turnover ratio, the gross profit percentage, and dozens of other ratios and analytical measures. In addition to updating that Excel spreadsheet, Nelson asked Bishop to design and prepare visual graphics for each major ratio and analytical measure to make it easier to quickly grasp major changes that were taking place in the company's operating results and financial condition.

Bishop had been pleasantly surprised over the previous two weeks that Nelson had identified several measures to improve not only the administration of the audit but also the performance of individual audit procedures. Plus, she had definitely taken control of the BRIC audit. At times, Bishop thought that she was a little too bossy, but, in his view, it was her prerogative to assert her authority. After her near-disastrous performance during the brainstorming session, Bishop had doubted that she had the necessary experience, maturity, and tenacity to supervise the fieldwork for an audit the size of the BRIC engagement, but her demeanor and performance since that session had caused him to rethink that assessment.

Despite his generally positive view of Nelson's leadership skills, Bishop still expected her to struggle at times on her first major supervisory assignment. Nelson appeared to be a classic micro-manager who was not proficient at delegating. She seemed to embrace the mantra "If you want it done right, do it yourself." While she kept Bishop busy with what he considered largely housekeeping tasks, she tackled all of the major planning tasks for the engagement without asking for his help or insight. Just as troubling was her perfectionist tendencies when it came to what Bishop considered minor details. On several occasions, Nelson had made it clear that she hated "sloppy" audit work papers; she expected every work paper to be a work of art. Granted, Bishop recognized that her interest in artistic work papers was likely a consequence of Cason Kellis's insistence that the BRIC work papers be "picture perfect."

The most important task that Nelson had completed over the previous two weeks was deciding how to allocate the year-end audit procedures to her subordinates. On every previous audit to which Bishop had been assigned that important task had been the responsibility of the audit engagement partner or the audit manager. But Cason Kellis had told Nelson that she could "go ahead and take care" of that task since she was familiar with the client and how the audit had been organized in the past.

In addition to Bishop's extensive administrative responsibilities for the audit, Nelson assigned him the responsibility for auditing BRIC's long-term debt and investment accounts and the corresponding revenue and expense accounts. Nelson assumed primary responsibility for leases, all the intangible asset accounts including goodwill, and the miscellaneous revenue and expense accounts that were not audited in tandem with a balance sheet account.

Nelson viewed the two most important accounts on the BRIC audit as inventory and accounts receivable because those accounts required the most time to audit and typically posed the most challenging accounting and financial reporting issues. She assigned the responsibility for those accounts to the two experienced staff accountants; Coleman Jackson would audit inventory, while Becky Linton would be responsible for accounts receivable. Linton would also audit accrued liabilities and accounts payable; Coleman's other major responsibility would be the property, plant and equipment accounts. While working on their assigned balance sheet accounts, Linton and Coleman would simultaneously audit the relevant "sister" accounts. For example, Linton would audit bad debt expense and the allowance for bad debts along with receivables, while Coleman would audit cost of goods sold and the allowance for inventory obsolescence simultaneously with inventory.

The client accounts that Nelson deemed to be of secondary importance she assigned to either herself or Bishop. Those accounts included, among many others, cash, prepaid expenses, and the stockholders' equity accounts. Although Nelson or Bishop would have the final responsibility for those accounts, most of the audit work related to them would be completed by one of the four rookie staff accountants. Bishop, for example, technically had responsibility for BRIC's cash accounts, but most of the audit procedures for those accounts, such as testing bank reconciliations and preparing and clearing bank confirmations, would be performed by a rookie. The four rookies would also be completing much of the tedious audit work necessary for the major accounts such as the various clerical tests of mathematical accuracy.

Nelson assigned the remaining audit tasks jointly to herself and Bishop. Those tasks included, among others, the search for subsequent events, the preparation of attorneys' letters, and obtaining the letter of representations. Whichever one of them had sufficient free time near the end of the audit would complete those tasks—Bishop assumed that Nelson would complete all or the majority of those tasks.

In her role as the supervising audit senior, Nelson would function as the immediate supervisor of Bishop, the two experienced staff accountants, and the four rookie staff accountants on the BRIC audit team. Nelson asked Bishop to help resolve any major problems that the staff accountants encountered on their assignments when she was busy or otherwise unavailable.

When Nelson completed the task assignments for the BRIC audit, she asked Bishop to review and comment on them. Those assignments were displayed on a document that she referred to as the "Matrix," which was an elaborate four-color diagram that she planned to post on the wall of the audit conference room. Instead of input on the document, Bishop got the impression that Nelson was fishing for a compliment when she handed it to him.

Bishop's first reaction after glancing at the document was one of surprise. Because of his experience level, he had expected Nelson to assign him responsibility for either accounts receivable or inventory, the two most challenging client accounts. Instead, she had assigned him two accounts, long-term debt and investments, that typically were not that difficult to audit. He was also surprised that the "Matrix" overlooked what in his mind was clearly the most important BRIC account, namely, sales revenue. He scanned the document twice searching for that account but it was nowhere to be found.

When Bishop asked Nelson why she hadn't assigned the sales account to any-one, she was obviously peeved. It was apparent that she hadn't expected, and did not appreciate, any criticism, even deserved criticism, of her masterpiece.

"Oh … well … well, of course, it goes without saying that … that Becky will be responsible for that account," she responded as her face betrayed equal por-tions of surprise, embarrassment, and resentment. "Many of the audit objec-tives for the year-end accounts receivable tests overlap with those of sales, so, of course, Becky will take responsibility for that account. And I will have her per-form the other year-end sales tests including the cutoff tests, the various sub-stantive analytical tests for that account, and so on and so forth."

In fact, Bishop's experience on most audits had been that the sales revenue ac-count was, strangely enough, an orphan account. Accounts receivable, inven-tory, and accrued liabilities typically garnered much more attention and a much larger proportion of the total audit budget than sales.

Bishop realized that the orphan status of the sales account was a consequence of the balance sheet mentality that had permeated the audit strategies of the major accounting firms for decades. He was aware that during the early twenti-eth century the balance sheet was typically the only financial statement formally audited. Even as the importance of determining and reporting a periodic net in-come or loss for companies became evident over time, auditors continued to or-ganize their audits from a balance sheet perspective. Audit tests applied to revenue and expense accounts were largely treated as offshoots or by-products of the audit procedures applied to the related balance sheet accounts. So, ironically, the responsibility for auditing sales revenue, the account most likely to be im-pacted by a financial statement fraud, was often treated as an afterthought—à la Emma Nelson. Bishop thought that was particularly foolhardy on an engage-ment such as the BRIC audit where management seemed to have a much stronger than normal incentive to overstate the company's revenues.

Another informal assignment that Nelson had given Bishop since the brain-storming session was to "press the flesh," as she called it. She wanted Bishop to spend time becoming acquainted with the client accounting personnel with whom the audit team would be working. Nelson told Bishop that good working relationships with the client's accounting staff were critical to the successful com-pletion of an audit—something he already knew, of course. At the time, Bishop realized that Nelson was subtly suggesting that he needed to improve his inter-personal skills.

Day by day, Bishop made it a point to introduce himself to one or more of BRIC's key accounting personnel including the divisional controllers, the individual ac-countants who had direct responsibility for major accounts such as inventory and accounts receivable, the director of internal audit, and the accounting department's secretarial staff. During the audit planning session in late October, Bishop had met some of those individuals, but those meetings had involved nothing more than handshakes and exchanges of hellos.

Nelson told Bishop that it was particularly important that he get to know Bud Wallace, who oversaw BRIC's accounting department, because she and Wallace had "poor chemistry." She was hoping that Bishop would develop a "man-to-man" relationship with Wallace that would prove beneficial for her and the entire audit team.

Wallace was an articulate, sturdy six-footer who always wore a tailored business suit, white button-down shirt, and tie while working. Bishop guessed that Wallace was in his late thirties and was not a native Midwesterner since there was a barely noticeable southern "twang" to certain words that he spoke. From the first time that Bishop interacted with Wallace, the two of them seemed to be comfortable with each other despite having very different personalities. While Bishop was serious and reserved, Wallace was gregarious and outgoing.

The second time that Bishop dropped by Wallace's office, the two of them became involved in a spirited discussion of whether the United States should move away from GAAP and adopt International Financial Reporting Standards (IFRS). Wallace had expressed a preference for adopting IFRS, while Bishop had played the role of devil's advocate and defended GAAP. Bishop didn't have a strong opinion either way; he had taken the position in support of GAAP because it was evident that Wallace enjoyed a lively debate.

A few days later, Wallace came to the audit conference room and invited Bishop to go on break with him. The ninth floor of BRIC's headquarters building had an impressive break room that included a large bank of well-stocked vending machines, a soda and espresso bar, and a large assortment of luxurious chairs, love seats, and even a few oversized recliners. The layout of the break room provided considerable privacy for one-on-one conversations.

During the fifteen-minute break, Wallace engaged Bishop in a free-flowing discussion of the role and responsibilities of the PCAOB. By this time, it had become clear to Bishop that Wallace enjoyed his company. Bishop also got the strange impression that Wallace was sizing him up for some reason. It was almost as if Wallace wanted something from Bishop. What exactly that was, Bishop had no idea.

Late in the afternoon of December 2, Emma Nelson called Bishop from another client's office and asked him to meet her at a midtown restaurant for dinner that evening. Nelson, who had spent most of the day at the other client helping an audit manager wrap up a quarterly review, said she wanted to finalize the year-end audit program for the BRIC audit.

On previous BRIC audits, the year-end audit program had been completed by the end of October and Nelson was anxious to get the final draft to Cason

Kellis and Jim Wilmeth for their review and approval. The completion of the final draft of the audit program was a major milestone in an audit engagement, although a few subsequent changes were typically made after the results of the internal control tests and the analytical procedures performed for planning purposes were available.

"Michael, don't tell anyone, but one reason I want to meet tonight is so that I can check out Bienvenuti's, which just opened a few weeks ago," Nelson confessed to Bishop while they were on the phone. "Since we are going to be discussing business, we can charge the dinner off to our expense accounts."

Bishop knew that he and Nelson could have easily spent an hour or two on Tuesday morning finalizing the audit program. Plus, he didn't think that Nelson's interest in Bienvenuti's was genuine because she clearly wasn't a "foodie." So, there had to be some reason that Nelson wanted to speak with him privately.

"Hi Michael, I showed up a little early so that we could get a good table," Nelson said cheerfully after a waiter had escorted him to a secluded table in the rear of the restaurant where she was seated.

"Well, I do love Italian food so I can't wait to see the menu," Bishop responded.

For well over an hour, both before and during their meal, Nelson and Bishop discussed several wide-ranging topics related to the BRIC audit. Nelson began by expressing her concern over the internal control testing for the engagement.

On a couple of occasions, Nelson had dropped in on Paula Henderson and asked how the control tests were going. In each case, Henderson had seemed frazzled and confused: frazzled because she realized that she and her team were weeks behind schedule and confused because she couldn't recall being on an audit where the internal control tests were effectively divorced from the remainder of the audit.

The previous week, Henderson had asked Nelson point blank how the year-end substantive tests could be started well before the internal control testing was completed. Nelson had told her that Cason Kellis was most concerned with determining the effectiveness of BRIC's internal controls over financial reporting as required by Section 404 of the Sarbanes-Oxley Act. Assessing control risk to determine the nature, timing, and extent of year-end substantive audit tests was only a secondary concern of Kellis. The explanation had obviously not satisfied Henderson but she had chosen not to pursue the matter with Nelson.

"I really didn't know what to tell her, to be honest," Nelson explained to Bishop. "I thought I had to tell her something and that seemed as reasonable as anything. The fact of the matter is, I really don't know why Cason has decided to separate the internal control tests from the rest of the audit." After a brief pause, Nelson continued. "It seems to me that it is going to be very messy to try to change the planned year-end substantive tests in mid-January after we finally have all of the results of the internal control tests. Don't you agree?"

"Uh, yeah. Sure. Absolutely." Bishop was much more interested in Bienvenuti's impressive menu than he was with Cason Kellis's irrational internal control testing strategy for the BRIC audit.

"You would think that Cason or Wilmeth would at least explain the reasoning for this strange approach. Wouldn't you?"

"Well, Emma, they probably have a plan or strategy, but, for some reason, they don't want to share it with you at this point."

Because of his conversation with Jim Wilmeth at Cason Kellis's Halloween party, Bishop realized that the audit partner's plan was to treat the internal control tests as a necessary evil and ignore their results for purposes of selecting and designing the year-end substantive tests. Because Nelson was naive, Bishop didn't think that she would believe him if he provided that explanation, which was why he didn't.

Nelson next asked Bishop if he had made progress in updating the Excel spreadsheet containing the quarter-by-quarter analysis of BRIC's key financial ratios. Bishop had updated the spreadsheet through the third quarter and planned to calculate the fourth-quarter ratios as soon as the year-end working trial balance was available.

"What do the ratios look like? Do there seem to be any developing or worsening trends in them?" Nelson asked.

Nelson was aware that several of BRIC's key ratios had been very weak over the past couple of years despite the impressive operating results reported by the company. During the previous several months, she had performed most of the work on the quarterly reviews of BRIC's financial statements, but she had only spot-checked the company's financial ratios during those reviews.

"Well, the inventory and receivables turnover ratios did weaken over the first three quarters of the year," Bishop explained hesitantly. He was reluctant to discuss the negative trends that he had discovered in BRIC's key ratios because Nelson might be upset that he had not yet brought them to her attention.

"Oh, wow, that's not good. Those ratios were already weak and if they are getting worse, I may have to talk to Cason about increasing the scope of the year-end tests of inventory and receivables."

Once again, Nelson's naivete was evident. Bishop was certain that no matter the outcome of the internal control tests or the preliminary analytical procedures, Kellis wasn't going to increase the rigor or the scope of the year-end substantive tests.

"I hate to mention this, Michael, but, I am a little concerned with how this audit is uh … uh … developing, I guess I would say. The past three years, the audit partner and manager were much more involved in the audit by this point. It is kind of surprising that I have heard almost nothing from either Cason or Jim Wilmeth during the past two weeks."

Bishop hoped that for the first time Nelson would directly criticize her superiors, who clearly deserved that criticism. But she didn't.

"I know what Cason has in mind. He has a lot of faith in me, and so he has decided to give me a much larger share of the responsibility for the audit than the supervising audit seniors have had in the past." Nelson paused to collect her thoughts. "What concerns me a little, though, is that I sometimes wonder if I am really ready for that much responsibility." Nelson added with an uneasy laugh, "You don't know how difficult it is for me to admit that."

Bishop took a long drink of tea while hoping that he wouldn't have to respond to any of Nelson's statements. It was obvious to him that Nelson had no clue that Kellis and Wilmeth held the BRIC audit in contempt and had little interest in it. She was also unaware that she would be served up as the sacrificial lamb by the two of them if the audit blew up.

After a lengthy silence, Bishop decided he had to say something.

"Well, Emma, this is your fourth year on the audit and you have been progressing at a fast pace, so it only stands to reason that Kellis would have a lot of faith in you. And, of course, it's normal for everyone to experience a little self-doubt occasionally."

Bishop was a master at concealing his true thoughts and at crafting seemingly sincere statements when he couldn't be more insincere. Such deception, which Bishop used to keep others at arm's length both emotionally and psychologically, seldom triggered any regret or remorse on his part. But, in this instance, he actually felt some degree of guilt for being less than candid with Nelson. There was no doubt that she had her faults but that was true of everyone. Bishop realized that she deserved better than having an indifferent wingman on an audit that could prove to be detrimental, if not disastrous, to her professional career, to say nothing of her self-confidence.

"Well, thank you, Michael. I really appreciate that," she replied earnestly, which caused Bishop's guilt to deepen. "I know we got off to kind of a rough start, but I think that we are developing into a good team."

Later in the evening, after the two auditors' conversation regarding the details of the BRIC audit had waned considerably, Nelson nervously cleared her throat and then took a sip of wine. It was clear to Bishop that she was finally going to address the subject that had prompted her to invite him to the restaurant.

"I would like to bring up something that is, uh, a little, uh, embarrassing for me." After another sip of wine to bolster her courage, Nelson continued. "I want to thank you for not mentioning the fact that John Kelly and I are ... I mean were ... seeing each other. That was very sweet of you. I know that I don't need to say this, but I would very much appreciate it if you don't mention that to anyone in the future as well."

Bishop's sixth sense told him two things: one, Nelson was, in fact, extremely grateful that he had not mentioned her relationship with Kelly to anyone; and two, she was lying when she suggested that the relationship had ended.

"Because John is assigned to the BRIC audit, I understand that it would be inappropriate for us to be seeing each other." She hastily added, "Of course, it's not like we are working together, but I know that we will be interacting to some degree."

"Hey Emma. Don't worry about it. I haven't mentioned anything to anybody and I won't."

"Well, thank you, again, Michael."

Nelson hurriedly changed the topic of the conversation. "Wow, look at that. I had no idea it was that late. You know what, why don't we meet first thing tomorrow morning in the conference room and hammer out the final draft of the audit program? Is that okay with you?"

"Absolutely. That pasta made me sleepy. I need to head home and climb in the sack," Bishop replied with a fake yawn.

Fifteen minutes later, Bishop unlocked the door to his apartment and walked inside. Other than a TV, an old couch from his college days, an unmade bed in the far corner of the room, and the nightstand next to the bed, the living room/bedroom of his studio apartment was unfurnished. And the walls were totally bare, except for one small framed photo, a photo that couldn't be seen from most of the room because it was hidden from view by the lamp that sat atop the nightstand.

After lying down in his bed, Bishop began aimlessly flipping through dozens of TV channels trying to find something that was at least marginally entertaining. Ten minutes later, he gave up, turned off the TV and tossed the remote control on the nightstand. Bishop turned on his side and paused as he spent several moments studying the photo, a ritual that he repeated every night. Then, he reached up and switched off the light and hoped that he would fall asleep quickly and peacefully.

Chapter 6

Monday, December 16

"Emma, could I speak to you for a few minutes?" Paula Henderson asked after stepping into the audit conference room where Emma Nelson and Michael Bishop were hard at work.

Although it was mid-December, Jim Wilmeth had spent no more than a handful of hours in the audit conference room. Nelson and Bishop had not seen Cason Kellis at BRIC headquarters since the late October meeting in which Suzanne Jennings had berated the audit team.

"Sure, Paula. What's up?" Nelson replied.

Henderson paused for a few moments after glancing at Bishop who was studying an Excel spreadsheet on his laptop computer.

Sensing that Henderson wanted to speak about something privately, Nelson asked her if she wanted to go to the break room where they could "chat."

"Oh. No. I guess that's not necessary. We are all on the same team here," Henderson responded. "At least, we are supposed to be," she added with a wry chuckle, referring to the fact that she didn't feel as if she was a full-fledged member of the BRIC audit team.

"Okay. Well, what would you like to talk about?" Nelson asked. Nelson's words betrayed the fact that she was busy and wanted Henderson to get to the point, and quickly.

"Well, I wanted to ask Jim about this issue, but he hasn't been around recently, at least I haven't seen him."

When Henderson paused again, Nelson flashed a toothy but insincere smile while she nodded her head vigorously, signaling for Henderson to continue, and quickly.

"I've been having trouble getting the client to cooperate," Henderson said. "We are missing documents on several of the internal control tests that we are doing and the client employees who are supposed to be helping us are dragging their feet in getting them to us."

"So, do you want me to speak to someone?" Nelson asked, implying with her tone of voice that doing so wasn't her responsibility but rather Henderson's.

"Well, again, I would normally ask Jim Wilmeth about this because I think that he is the one who I'm supposed to be communicating with, but—"

"Jim isn't here, obviously," a now annoyed Nelson said, finishing Henderson's sentence.

No doubt, by this point, Henderson regretted having made the trek to the audit conference room from the third-floor dungeon where she and her troops were stationed.

"Well, I just wanted your professional opinion, I guess." Henderson, a matronly woman in her early thirties who looked like she should have been teaching a first-grade class rather than working as an independent auditor, responded to the less than tactful Nelson by making a brave effort to become more forceful. "On this one test that we are trying to complete, we have obtained bills of lading for 154 of the 161 sales transactions that we selected for testing. The client's accounting clerks told us that they can't find the bills of lading for the other seven transactions in our sample and don't have the time to search for them now. So, my question is, do you think it would be okay to choose seven more sales transactions at random to replace the ones for which the client can't find the shipping documents?"

Michael Bishop, a master of multi-tasking, like most auditors, was eavesdropping on the conversation between Henderson and Nelson as he continued to scan the spreadsheet on his laptop computer. He was certain that despite her having been away from public accounting for several years, Henderson was well aware that you couldn't simply drop transactions or account balances selected for testing because the client couldn't or wouldn't produce the relevant documents. Bishop was just as certain that the indifferent attitude toward internal control testing exhibited by Cason Kellis had caused Henderson to suggest doing just that.

After a few moments of uneasy silence, Emma Nelson replied to Henderson's question. "Paula, I don't think that is a reasonable solution. In fact, that's not a solution at all." Nelson's words were framed with disapproval and condescension.

Henderson nodded in agreement as she looked at the floor, clearly embarrassed that she had suggested the possibility in the first place. The timid and mild-mannered Henderson then thanked Nelson before excusing herself and slipping quietly out of the conference room.

When Henderson was well out of earshot, Nelson asked rhetorically, "Can you believe that? I don't know how she could think that was acceptable. I wonder whose idea it was to hire her?"

Bishop felt sorry for Henderson. In just a few short weeks, the well-intentioned professional had joined the dark side. Time pressure, insolent superiors, and apathetic subordinates had caused her to adopt an "anything goes" attitude toward her assigned responsibilities.

On two occasions over the previous few weeks, Bishop had returned to the audit conference room to find Emma Nelson and John Kelly sitting side by side at the conference room table. As soon as he entered the room, the two lovebirds—that is, alleged former lovebirds—had abruptly shifted from a hushed tone of conversation to an energetic and ostentatious discussion related to the audit. In one of those staged discussions, Kelly had told Nelson that the use of floaters to perform much of the internal control testing was proving to be a major headache for Henderson. According to Kelly, the transient auditors didn't assume ownership of the tests because they didn't have complete responsibility for them—as many as three different auditors worked sequentially on a given test. Kelly also told Nelson that the recurring learning curves that had to be surmounted by the tag team of come-and-go auditors slowed down the tests and significantly increased Henderson's supervisory burden.

Henderson had certainly been given a tough and thankless assignment, but her own shortsightedness and stubbornness were making matters worse. More than a week earlier, Bishop and Henderson had spent 15 minutes together in the BRIC break room. As they sat there, Bishop had mentioned the prior year's summary ICFR (internal controls over financial reporting) memo that was included in the permanent work paper files. That memo discussed several significant deficiencies in internal controls that had been documented during the prior year audit. When it became apparent that Henderson was unaware of the memo, Bishop described the nature of those deficiencies and suggested that she review the memo before drafting the comparable memo for the current year's audit—Cason Kellis was responsible for the final version of the ICFR memo but almost certainly would rely heavily, if not completely, on Henderson's draft.

When Bishop completed his brief overview of the prior year ICFR memo, Henderson had immediately responded, "I'm so swamped by this year's internal control tests that I don't have time to go digging through the prior year work papers to see what the auditors did last year or what they found."

Because of the AWOL status of Jim Wilmeth, Emma Nelson had been completing tasks that Wilmeth would normally have performed, meaning that Bishop over the past two weeks had been forced to step in and help Becky Linton and Jackson Coleman on their assigned accounts. He had also spent time orienting the two rookie staff accountants who had begun their tours of duty on the BRIC audit. The other two rookies who had been assigned to the BRIC audit team were scheduled to arrive at the client's headquarters on Wednesday, December 18, which was just two days away.

Early one morning when Bishop noticed that the verbally challenged Linton seemed to be struggling with the task of choosing the individual receivables accounts to be confirmed, he offered to help her. The relevant prior year work papers were difficult for Linton to use as a road map because they were not well organized. At first, Linton seemed to suggest that she didn't need any help—at least that was what Bishop gathered from the series of nods, grimaces, and other nonverbal gestures displayed by Linton. But then, she relented and accepted Bishop's offer of assistance. A short while later, the two of them were actually exchanging brief oral statements.

Linton was adept at using the accounting firm's software application to select the large random sample of small customer account balances to be confirmed via negative confirmations. But she was having difficulty deciding how to choose a judgmental sample from the client's larger receivables—Jim Wilmeth had insisted on sending positive confirmations to those customers despite his suggestion to the contrary during the heated exchange he had with Cason Kellis during the brainstorming session. Linton was also stymied by the task of deciding which of the two dozen or so "problem" accounts should be confirmed. Problem accounts were those receivables that were in litigation.

Bishop first helped Linton identify a set of quantitative and qualitative factors to use in choosing the large receivables accounts to confirm. Next, he told Linton to discuss each of the problem accounts with the client's assistant credit manager, an affable and helpful accountant who he had met the previous week—BRIC's credit manager was nearing retirement, gruff, self-absorbed, and verbally abusive to both his subordinates and to auditors. Bishop suggested that Linton develop a bullet list of the problem accounts that included brief descriptions of the underlying disputes that had led to litigation. When she completed that list, Bishop told her that they would review the accounts and decide what additional audit evidence, if any, was needed for each of them.

Following their 30-minute meeting, Linton apologized to Bishop for taking up so much of his time. Bishop responded by encouraging her to come to him when she had questions. "Becky, we are working on this audit together. Any time you have a question or are stumped by some issue, come to the conference room and I will drop what I am working on and we will solve the problem together."

A few days earlier, Bishop had spent several hours working with Jackson Coleman. The effusive and overly confident Coleman had also resisted Bishop's initial offer of help. Late one evening, however, Coleman came to Bishop with a series of questions regarding the tricky LIFO accounting procedures applied by BRIC. Bishop was well versed in those procedures because another of his clients used the same variation of LIFO. The two of them became so engrossed in discussing and dissecting the unusual approach to applying LIFO that they lost track of the time. At 10 p.m., the night shift janitorial crew walked into the audit conference room and interrupted Bishop and his attentive and very grateful student.

Although Bishop was not the supervising audit senior for the BRIC audit, he realized that he would be spending a significant amount of his time supervising the staff accountants on the audit team while Emma Nelson served as the quasi-audit manager for the engagement. Plus, it had become obvious to Bishop over the past couple of weeks that Emma Nelson was not the most approachable supervisor. She was so wrapped up in her own assignments that she was often abrupt, if not downright rude, when the staff accountants came to her with questions.

Bishop found his new supervisory responsibilities strangely rewarding. At heart, he was a problem solver and he enjoyed helping staff accountants who were struggling with technical issues that had not been addressed in their college accounting courses—after graduation, Bishop had quickly discovered that his college accounting courses had provided him with only an introductory overview of most major accounting topics. Bishop also enjoyed the freedom that his supervisory responsibilities gave him. In the past, he had been expected to be either at his workspace or interacting with client personnel. But now, given his new role, he had the freedom to disappear for an hour or more before anyone even noticed that he was gone.

On this Monday evening, Bishop had a meeting scheduled with Bud Wallace to discuss audit scheduling issues for the inventory observation and accounts receivable confirmation audit procedures. Each of those audit tests had to be coordinated with the client because they required the involvement of several client employees. Nelson was supposed to have met with Wallace in the early afternoon to discuss those topics, but shortly before lunch she had asked Bishop to take her place because of a last minute "emergency" that had arisen. Bishop was convinced that Nelson had staged the emergency so that she wouldn't have to spend an uncomfortable hour or so with Wallace who she obviously disliked for some reason.

When Bishop dropped by Wallace's office that afternoon, the accounting manager had seemed pleasantly surprised that he would be discussing the audit scheduling issues with him rather than Nelson. After a few brief exchanges, Wallace told Bishop that he was busy working on a report that Suzanne Jennings needed that afternoon. He then asked Bishop if the two of them could meet that evening. Wallace suggested the Grotto, an upscale bar frequented by young business professionals.

The idea of meeting with Wallace after work in a bar was not appealing to Bishop since he didn't drink. Also unsettling was the fact that Wallace seemed intent on developing a friendship with him. At this point in his life, Bishop wasn't in the market for any serious friendships.

As the seconds had ticked by and Wallace waited for a response regarding the meeting he had suggested at the Grotto, Bishop hadn't been able to come up with any viable reason to turn down the invitation. So, he had chosen the only route available to him: capitulation.

"Well, okay. Sure, Bud," Bishop replied as enthusiastically as possible. "What time do want to meet?"

"Let's make it seven sharp," Wallace responded gleefully. "Surely you guys will have put away your work papers for the night by then."

Bishop was taken aback by the depth of Wallace's joy. It was as if Wallace had just made a date with the prom queen.

As Bishop walked away from Wallace's office, he wondered exactly what type of relationship Wallace wanted to develop with him. He hoped that the accounting manager wasn't looking for a new BFF.

"Hey Michael, belly up to the bar and let me buy you a drink," Wallace said to Bishop as the audit senior approached him that evening in the Grotto.

As the two shook hands, Bishop apologetically explained to Wallace that his favorite drink was a Virgin Mary—a Bloody Mary sans vodka.

"Are you sure?" Wallace responded. "They have some fabulous drinks here that are guaranteed to give you no more than a slight buzz."

"Well, maybe later, Bud. But I think I'll start with a Virgin Mary." After a brief pause, Bishop added, "If our scintillating discussion of inventory observations and receivables confirmations drags on too long, though, I just may have to loosen up and break out the whiskey." The two men shared a hearty laugh as Bishop loosened his necktie and then took off his suit jacket and laid it on the bar stool next to him.

For 15 minutes or more, Wallace and Bishop bounced from one subject to another in the sports world. At one point, Wallace, a fan of the local NBA team, invited Bishop to attend a game in the near future. BRIC Industries had a large corporate suite at the downtown arena where the team played. One of Wallace's job perks was a pair of tickets for eight games each season.

"You know, Michael, I can easily get my hands on a couple of more tickets if you want to bring your wife or girlfriend and make it a double date. I don't have a steady girlfriend, but I think I could scare up a date for the night."

"Oh, well, I don't know," Bishop responded as he struggled again to come up with a reasonable excuse to reject another cordial invitation extended by Wallace. "The next couple of months we are going to be working some really long hours. When I finally put away the laptop for the night in the middle of busy season, I just like to head home and crash in front of the TV."

"Okay, okay. I get it. I get it. You're one of those by-the-book 'professionals.' You're afraid that your sacred auditor independence might be compromised if someone saw you hanging out in the BRIC box down at the arena." The teasing tone of Wallace's voice revealed that he wasn't offended by Bishop's rejection of his offer. "Hey, if you change your mind, let me know."

Wallace shifted the topic of conversation away from sports. He asked Bishop for his thoughts on an ongoing political scandal that had been usurping the front pages of the metro daily the past couple of weeks. It was apparent to Bishop that Wallace had little interest in that topic himself and that he was only using it as a weak segue to another topic.

"I tell you one thing, they couldn't give those two crooks long enough prison sentences to suit me," Wallace observed a few minutes later, signaling the end to the snippet of conversation involving an embezzlement scheme masterminded by two city councilmen.

"Speaking of crooks," Wallace said intently before taking a drink of his fresh gin and tonic, "I want to ask you a serious question, Michael." Bishop realized that Wallace was finally broaching the subject that he wanted to discuss. "Since my divorce a few years ago, I've had a lot of time to spend on my two hobbies. One of those is NBA basketball—as you now know. The other is the stock market." Wallace hesitated to stir his mixed drink. Bishop sensed that he was nervous for some reason. "I've always been fascinated by the stock market but never really had the time to study it and try to get my mind around it until the past few years."

Bishop sat silently as Wallace paused and once again stirred his drink. He was waiting for Wallace's "serious question." By this point, Bishop had decided that Wallace had a preplanned agenda for their meeting, an agenda that didn't involve discussing audit scheduling issues.

"I'm not sure how to ask this. I mean, this is just out of the blue." Finally, Wallace blurted out, "Do you think the stock market is rigged? You know, I mean, do you think it's a, uh, fair game, so to speak?" After a quick shot of gin and tonic, Wallace added, "Basically, what I'm asking is, do you think that crooked corporate executives and their buddies on Wall Street are scamming all of the rest of us investors by thumbing their collective noses at the securities laws, the SEC, and law enforcement authorities?"

After asking the question, Wallace stared directly at Bishop, studying his face for several moments, which made Bishop wonder exactly where Wallace was going with the new topic of conversation. Because he was now curious, Bishop decided to play along.

"Well … let me see. Do I think the stock market is rigged?" Bishop repeated Wallace's original question to give him a few extra moments to choose a tack to take in the mind game that he was now playing with the accounting manager. "Yeah, sure. I mean, I don't think there is any doubt that there are some parties that have always had a big advantage over other investors. And sometimes those parties, which certainly include corporate executives, play outside the rules that you and I and other small-time investors have to abide by."

Although he had included himself in the fraternity of "small-time investors," Bishop didn't have a dime invested in the stock market. After three-plus years in public accounting, he was still paying off his student loans from college and didn't have any extra cash to invest.

As Bishop was speaking, Wallace's face lit up. Wallace was clearly elated to hear Bishop's point of view on the subject at hand. As their conversation continued, it became apparent that Wallace was preoccupied by the regulation—

or lack thereof—of the stock market. He was convinced that the SEC was inept and was not doing an adequate job of policing the securities markets. He felt strongly that the SEC's incompetence had allowed dishonest corporate executives and big institutional investors on Wall Street to run roughshod over smaller investors.

"I tell you, it really burns me up when I read the enforcement cases settled by the SEC," Wallace began one of his rants. "Have you ever read any of the SEC's enforcement releases?"

"No. Can't say that I have," Bishop responded honestly.

"If you go back and review the fraud cases that the SEC has investigated in recent years, most of them were settled with the SEC doing nothing more than issuing a cease-and-desist order against the crooks that were responsible for the fraud. These corporate executives are lying in their financial statements to pump up their companies' stock prices and to make sure that their stock options get in the money. And then, when they get caught red-handed in a major accounting fraud, they offload the responsibility to someone else and wind up receiving no more than a slap on the wrist from the SEC." Wallace shook his head angrily. "After everything is said and done, the little guys, the small-time investors are left holding the bag."

Bishop was surprised by Wallace's statement and the degree of conviction with which he delivered it. What he found surprising and ironic was that Wallace, himself, from all indications, was window dressing BRIC's financial statements and, in doing so, propping up the company's stock price.

"What do you think, Michael?" Wallace continued. "You're an auditor. Your job is to search for management fraud. So, maybe you have a more informed opinion than I do. Am I off base?"

Bishop's first thought was to turn the tables on Wallace and ask him why he was fudging BRIC's financial data. But Bishop realized that might anger, if not enrage, Wallace. Bishop knew that self-righteous individuals were often blind to their own transgressions. Then again, Wallace seemed to be a rational individual. Bishop was almost certain that rather than being self-righteous and blind to his own bad behavior, Wallace was effectively confessing that he was appalled by the aggressive accounting that he was being coaxed or forced to apply by his superiors.

Instead of suggesting that BRIC and Wallace were guilty of creative accounting, Bishop chose to take a safer route in responding to his question.

"Well, yeah, I agree with you that the SEC doesn't go out of its way to punish crooked corporate executives, at least from what I've read in the *Wall Street Journal* and other business publications," Bishop replied. As an afterthought he added, "And, I think that may encourage other corporate executives to fiddle with their companies' numbers, which, in turn, creates headaches for everyone, including accountants, auditors, regulators, and, probably more than anyone else, the so-called 'little' investors."

"Exactly," Wallace responded as he carelessly slammed his empty drink glass down on the top of the bar. "Someone needs to teach these corporate con artists a real lesson or the problem is going to get worse and worse and worse." Wallace accented each "worse" by striking the top of the bar with his closed right fist.

Bishop attempted to quell Wallace's mounting anger and emotion by diverting his attention from corrupt corporate executives to independent auditors.

"Well, Bud, I guess that's where auditors, like me, are supposed to come into play. I mean, in a sense, we're the appointed whistleblowers for the financial reporting world."

Wallace shook his head disgustedly. "No offense, Michael, but based upon my experience, auditors are not doing their jobs. Understand, I'm not attacking you personally. You're kind of like me. You're just a foot soldier taking orders from your superiors. Who I hold responsible are guys like your boss, that candy-ass Kellis character. During that meeting a few weeks ago, Kellis allowed Jennings to steamroll him. It was almost as if she warned him that he had better back off when it came to auditing our accounting records."

Wallace stopped long enough to order his third drink of the evening. Then, he leaned toward Bishop and quietly but forcefully delivered a startling confession embedded in a set of angry accusations. "Michael, here's the plain, simple, unvarnished truth. My boss is a crook. Your boss is a self-interested weasel. And, worst of all, we do whatever they tell us to do. Why? Because we are too damn pathetic to stand up for what is right."

Bishop was dumbfounded. Never in his three-plus years of public accounting had he faced a set of circumstances even remotely similar to the situation he faced at that moment. His client's primary financial accountant, the person who was effectively in charge of its external financial reporting function, had just admitted, in so many words, that he was "cooking the books" of his employer.

As he sat there on the bar stool staring straight ahead, Bishop steadied himself, not allowing himself to display any observable reaction to Wallace's staggering statements.

Wallace realized that despite appearing to be composed, Bishop had to be stunned by what he had just heard. Instead of recanting those statements, Wallace became even more adamant.

"I know you're wondering what in the hell is going on here," Wallace said as he leaned in even closer to Bishop and lowered his voice even more. "I mean, what in the hell am I doing talking to you about this stuff?" Wallace didn't wait for Bishop to make an effort to answer his rhetorical question. "Here's the deal.

I've watched you and interacted with you enough to know that you aren't the typical fast-track, boot-licking auditor. I'm pretty sure that you realize that most of the work you do is useless. Hell, even when you guys find something that's wrong in our accounting records, you come up with some excuse to walk away from it. I bet that doesn't happen just on our audits. I'm guessing that you have seen that happen time after time on the jobs that you have worked on."

Wallace turned away from Bishop. After guzzling down his third gin and tonic, he put down his empty drink glass and shoved it to the side as he motioned for the bartender to bring him another drink.

"Well, Mr. Bishop, looks like the cat has got your tongue. No comment? Lost interest in our conversation all of a sudden?"

Wallace's words were spoken in anger. Bishop wasn't sure how much of that anger was fueled by alcohol and how much was fueled by Wallace's deep-seated resentment of corporate executives, Wall Street fat cats, and independent auditors, such as himself.

Following a long and uncomfortable pause, Wallace turned back to face Bishop, who continued to sit motionless, staring straight ahead. "I want to tell you something," Wallace began in an almost solemn but still angry tone. "When I was growing up as a kid in Michigan, my old man worked for Burford & Neill, the large manufacturing company that supplies automotive parts to the Big Three automakers. From every one of his paychecks, eight percent was deducted for his 401(k) plan. He believed in that company and he wanted to invest in it and grow with it. So, every one of those 401(k) dollars he invested in Burford & Neill's common stock." Wallace paused just long enough to once again signal the bartender that he wanted another drink.

"After he had put in thirty-plus years with the company, along comes this hotshot new management team that was hellbent on transforming Burford & Neill into a New Age operation. That new management team began tinkering with the company's old school but rock solid business model and began making huge side bets on mortgage-backed securities and other wild-ass financial derivatives. For a while, their ideas seemed to be working. They got the company's stock price up and then cashed in a huge wad of stock options that the board had given them. And then, the house of cards began collapsing. The company began suffering large losses, but those losses weren't reported because top management ordered their accountants to cover them up. It only took them five years to run the company into the ground. And the guys on your team, Burford & Neill's auditors, concealed the fact that the company was going down the tubes by issuing clean opinions every year on their financial statements."

Wallace stopped speaking long enough to study Bishop's face and make sure that he was listening intently.

"Then, as you probably know, the accounting fraud was revealed by a whistle-blower, an internal auditor. Some young lady two years out of college who had the decency and courage to do what was right. Three months later, just a few months after your Big Four cousins had issued a clean opinion on the company's last set of annual financial statements, Burford & Neill was declared bankrupt and placed under the control of a receiver by a federal judge. And guess what? My Dad's 401(k) went from a value of $410,000 to zero. Now, Mom and Dad have to scrape by living off their monthly Social Security checks."

Because Wallace was beginning to choke up, he stopped briefly to gain control of his emotions.

"Two months ago, Dad got a job as a greeter at the local WalMart. You know why? Because he needed to make some money so that he and Mom could buy Christmas gifts for the grandkids this year."

As Wallace told his father's sad story, Bishop's guilt by association had slowly mounted. He was sorry for Wallace's father. He was sorry for all the hard-working but financially naive investors who had bet their life savings on a company for which they had worked all their lives only to lose some or all of those savings when the company's stock price nosedived following the disclosure of an accounting fraud. It was an all-too common occurrence. And Wallace was spot on for suggesting that auditors shouldered much of the responsibility for the plights of those individuals.

There was no doubt in Bishop's mind that it would be impossible to totally eradicate fraudulent accounting schemes regardless of the amount of political and economic resources committed to that goal. Because fraud is a natural by-product of any economic system, capitalistic or otherwise, independent auditors had been given the critical responsibility of serving as the final line of defense against dishonest executives. Unfortunately, auditors all too often refused, or otherwise failed, to carry out that role.

Two to three minutes passed before Wallace spoke again. "After Jennings and her boys took over BRIC, they had these great plans that were supposedly going to revive the company, to get it back on track. But they couldn't. So, she began telling me what she wanted. Each quarter, she decides what earnings number to report and then me and my boys have to do whatever it takes to make sure we reach it."

Wallace paused and looked away as if overcome by guilt and shame. After taking a deep breath, he continued.

"Holding the books open at the end of the quarter to overstate sales, creating fake inventory, understating accruals. You name it, we do it. When the former divisional controllers wouldn't go along with her grand scheme, she fired them one by one and then told me to find replacements for them from our large slush pile of job applications. She told me to find applicants who were more 'open-minded,' to use her expression."

Wallace quaffed down more than half of his fresh drink. "Funny thing is, at the same time that Burford & Neill's accountants were painting a rosy picture of that company's operating results, we were doing the exact same thing at BRIC." Wallace laughed cynically. "When Jennings was over there in Europe near the end of the third quarter, we got our wires crossed and wound up missing our consensus earnings forecast for that quarter by a couple of cents. Man, was she ticked off. She was even more ticked off when the stock price plunged fifteen per cent. Damn, I almost got fired over that."

As Wallace retrieved his wallet and then laid a credit card on the bar, Bishop stood and began putting on his jacket.

"Before you leave, Michael, let me finish the story."

Bishop reluctantly sat back down on the bar stool next to Wallace.

"I have a plan. I'm going to share that plan with you because I think I can trust you. I think you have a conscience. I think you want to do what is right, kind of like that internal auditor at Burford & Neill."

As Wallace stared at Bishop, the young auditor never flinched, never changed his facial expression.

"BRIC is not going to make the number that Jennings wants for the fourth quarter, which she already told me is fifty-nine cents per share. In fact, we are going to miss that number by a mile. But, this time, I'm going to make sure that the real accounting figures go to you guys and that the tables are turned on Jennings and Zimmer and Hakes." Wallace paused to take another deep breath and to bolster his resolve to continue. "This is where you come in. I need the auditors help. And you are the only one that I can trust. You are the only one in that outfit who has the strength of character and resolve to do the right thing."

Bishop wanted to leave but he couldn't. He wanted to hear the punch line of the incredible story he had just been told.

"Michael, your boss, Kellis, is the kind of guy who would help clients cover up bad news."

Bishop immediately thought of the oil and gas company client that had landed Kellis in hot water with the PCAOB.

"All that I'm asking is that you do your job," Wallace continued. "Even someone at your level on an audit team has the leverage to put the brakes on a client's accounting scam."

Bishop glanced over either shoulder and then made sure that the bartender was out of range before he responded under his breath. "What? What are you suggesting?"

Wallace ignored Bishop's question and instead focused exclusively on the role that he wanted Bishop to play in his plan. "If Kellis decides to help Jennings report the earnings number that she wants for the fourth quarter, I need you to somehow make sure that doesn't happen."

"So, in other words, you want me to be the point man in some grand conspiracy?" Bishop whispered. "Why don't you do the dirty work? Just go to the audit committee."

"Come on, Michael. You know better than that. You know that every member of our audit committee is a crony of Jennings or Zimmer or Hakes. Don't be ridiculous."

"Okay then, call the SEC and tell them that Jennings won't report the company's actual results."

"Michael. Michael. Believe me. It's not that simple. This is very complicated. I haven't handled this very well tonight. I may have blown it. Again, I know that you are honest and that you have a conscience. I know that you have as little respect for auditing and the SEC and crooked corporate executives as I do. You want to do the right thing." Wallace's voice now had a pleading tone to it. "I want you to meet again with me and a couple of the divisional controllers. I can arrange a meeting in our building. After we meet, then you can do whatever you believe is best." Wallace placed his hand on Bishop's shoulder. "Please, before you talk to anyone about what was said here tonight, meet with us and hear us out."

Bishop brushed Wallace's hand away and then slowly shook his head. His grandmother, who had spent her entire life on the Rosebud Indian Reservation on the desolate and windblown plains of South Dakota, had once told him that his life would be shaped by a handful of decisions that he would make, decisions that would define or redefine his future. He realized that he was likely facing such a decision.

Bishop adjusted the collar of his jacket and then tugged at the cuffs of his shirt, signaling that he was preparing to leave. After getting up from his bar stool, he asked in a soft but stern tone, "When can we meet?"

"I can arrange everything in one week. So, that would be next Monday, the twenty-third. Because the next day is Christmas Eve, the building will be deserted by 8 p.m. We could meet anytime after that. The meeting shouldn't require more than an hour."

As Bishop stared at Wallace, he noticed a gleam of hope flickering in his eyes.

"Okay," Bishop replied firmly and then headed toward the exit.

———————

Twenty minutes later, Bishop was sitting on the edge of his bed staring at his blank TV screen. Prior to meeting with Wallace, Bishop's life had a humdrum, monotonous routine to it. It had been boring and uneventful except for the occasional entertainment provided by the squad of dysfunctionalistas who made up the BRIC audit team. Now, regardless of what he decided to do, the next few months would be complicated. Instead of standing on the sidelines where he was comfortable, he was going to be involved in a messy, if not chaotic, set of circumstances. He wished that someone else had been chosen for this assignment, someone with a stronger sense of purpose and clarity.

As he continued to sit on his bed, wallowing in some degree of self-pity, Bishop recalled a letter that he had opened three years earlier during an audit of Jensen & Turner, Inc., a small software company whose stock was traded on the NASDAQ.

Because he was in charge of the correspondence file for that engagement, Bishop, a rookie staff accountant at the time, had opened the letter that was addressed to "Jensen and Turner Indepenent Audtors." The cursive script on the outside of the small envelope had been written by someone with not only impaired spelling skills but also poor penmanship. Those same shortcomings were evident throughout the one-page letter enclosed in the envelope. In the letter, an 88-year-old widow told how she had invested $14,473.21 in 400 shares of Jensen & Turner's common stock three years earlier—her nephew, a "date trader," according to the letter, had made the purchase for her. As bad luck would have it, the old lady had purchased the stock near the zenith of its price. Three years later, the price had collapsed to $.73 per share, meaning that her investment was worth approximately $300.

In her letter, the old lady said that she lived on a fixed income that consisted of her Social Security checks and the small monthly pension she received from her husband's former employer. Her letter mentioned how she had written five times to Jensen & Turner asking that her investment be returned. She explained that any "divvidens" due on the stock could be kept by the auditors or returned to the company or donated to the "Savation Army." She would be more than happy just to have her original investment returned.

At the time that Bishop was reading the letter, Jensen & Turner had been in Chapter 11 reorganization for more than nine months. The Chapter 11 bankruptcy filing would eventually be converted into a Chapter 7 filing. Upon liquidation, Jensen & Turner's unsecured creditors received ten cents on the dollar for their claims against the company; the company's stockholders received nothing.

Bishop had shown the letter to the Jensen & Turner audit engagement partner. After spending ten seconds quickly scanning the letter, the humorless partner had wadded it up and tossed it in a nearby trash can without saying a word.

Not surprisingly, Jensen & Turner's former creditors and stockholders filed a civil lawsuit against Bishop's employer, a lawsuit that was still working its way through the courts. Bishop had no idea whether his firm was culpable since he had served only as a "gofer" on the Jensen & Turner audit, but it was common knowledge among the members of the audit engagement team that the company had long used aggressive accounting practices to paint as favorable a picture of its financial health as possible. Similar to other financially troubled companies audited by Big Four accounting firms, the clean opinions that Bishop's firm had issued on Jensen & Turner's financial statements had given the company a veneer of respectability.

As he sat on his bed recalling the frail penmanship of Jensen & Turner's former stockholder, Michael Bishop turned and studied the photo of Ollie hanging on the wall to his left. A few seconds later after turning off the lamp next to Ollie's photo, Bishop, still fully clothed, rolled over and laid face down on his bed and tried to think of something other than Bud Wallace's father and the old lady with the poor penmanship.

Chapter 7

Friday, December 20

The past several days had been difficult ones for Michael Bishop. Since his unsettling encounter with Bud Wallace on Monday evening, he had spent hours considering his options. He planned to keep his word and meet with Wallace and the two divisional controllers the following Monday evening.

After the meeting on December 23, Bishop had no idea what he would do. He couldn't imagine that whatever happened during the meeting would have a significant impact on the decision he ultimately made. He assumed that the meeting would involve Wallace and the divisional controllers explaining their plan in more detail and then them asking him, if not pleading with him, to not divulge the plan to Cason Kellis. Bishop wasn't sure why it was so important to wait until the end of the fourth quarter to end the accounting fraud. Most likely, Wallace's plan included some way that he and his subordinates might be able to retain their jobs, or, at least, minimize the degree of responsibility they had to assume for the fraud. In either case, it was probably wishful thinking on Wallace's part.

Bishop felt sorry for Wallace and the divisional controllers, but, in a very real sense, they were responsible for the predicament in which they found themselves. By surrendering to the demands of BRIC's senior management, they had placed their professional lives and personal livelihoods in jeopardy. Now, they expected Bishop to help bail them out. That was a lot to ask of someone who they barely knew.

By his own admission, Bishop was a loner who didn't want to forfeit any measure of his private life in exchange for some degree of camaraderie, real or imagined. But he realized that he had become a member of a secret alliance headed up by a man of whom he knew very little. Because Wallace had belted down four drinks during their brief meeting, Bishop wondered if he had a serious drinking problem. On the other hand, Wallace's decision to confide in Bishop could have been a consequence of deep-seated emotional problems possibly linked to, or exacerbated by, the divorce he had mentioned or the sad plight of his father. Either possibility was disturbing.

The more Bishop thought about the situation he faced, the more he also became concerned by an issue that had not occurred to him during his tête-à-tête with Wallace at the Grotto, namely, the fact that he was now in possession of material "inside" information. He realized that if BRIC announced a huge fourth-quarter earnings miss, the company's stock price would drop sharply.

Bishop knew that certain brokerage firms specialized in selling "short" the stock of companies suspected of inflating their reported operating results. If such a company's earnings management or fraudulent accounting scheme was revealed, those brokerage firms could make a considerable profit by covering their short positions—that is, purchasing shares of the company's stock after the stock's price had plummeted. If someone knew for certain that an earnings manipulation scam would be "outed" in the near future, that someone could lock in a profit by shorting the given company's stock. That same someone could also face prosecution by federal law enforcement authorities since trading on inside information in such circumstances was patently illegal.

As the days passed, Bishop became increasingly uneasy with the fact that he was in possession of inside information that was literally worth tens of millions of dollars, if not more, possibly much more. He also recognized that a self-professed student of the stock market, such as Bud Wallace, would also be aware of the value of that information. Wallace had already confessed to being dishonest. So, it didn't require a stretch of one's imagination to consider the possibility that Wallace might attempt to profit from the fact that BRIC Industries' stock was speeding toward a proverbial brick wall. The same was true of the divisional controllers.

Bishop understood that corporate executives, corporate accountants, and even independent auditors were routinely in possession of inside information. The significant civil and criminal penalties for attempting to make a "quick buck" in the stock market by trading on that information were typically sufficient to discourage such behavior. Then again, Bishop had read of many cases in which corporate insiders had been prosecuted and received jail terms for engaging in insider trading. Some of those cases had involved independent auditors, including cases in which partners of Big Four accounting firms had profited from trading on inside information obtained from large public company clients.

Two days earlier, on late Wednesday afternoon, Wallace had dropped by the audit conference room. Finding Bishop alone, Wallace had stepped in and quietly told him that the meeting on the following Monday evening had been arranged and that Monday afternoon he would tell him exactly where the meeting would take place. At the time, Bishop thought of raising the inside information issue with Wallace, but he decided not to since he didn't want to take the chance of someone overhearing their conversation.

Three days earlier, on Tuesday morning, Wallace had come to the audit conference room when both Bishop and Nelson were present. After Wallace apologized to Bishop for spending their meeting in the Grotto "discussing everything but audit scheduling issues," the three of them had finalized the plans for the timing of the accounts receivable confirmation and inventory observation audit tests. As the three of them discussed the audit scheduling issues, Bishop had felt uncomfortable because he and Wallace were cooperating to conceal a shared secret from Nelson. Bishop's relationship with Wallace was clearly inconsistent with his responsibility to serve as an objective, third-party referee during the BRIC audit. For someone who had never been overly committed to the role and responsibilities of an independent auditor, Bishop missed the sense of personal and professional freedom that he now recognized was such an integral feature of that role and those responsibilities.

Another complication, a much more mundane complication that had been introduced in the past few days into Bishop's work environment was the presence of Jim Wilmeth. The audit manager had shown up unannounced on Wednesday morning and taken up residence in the audit conference room that essentially had been the exclusive domain of Bishop and Nelson until that point in time.

Bishop didn't have any problem being in Wilmeth's presence or interacting with him; the same could not be said of Emma Nelson. Since Wilmeth's arrival, the tension in the conference room had created the equivalent of a static electricity storm. When Wilmeth and Nelson spoke, stinging electrical charges flew in every direction. At first, the inability of the two to interact on any level beyond what one would expect of two seven-year-olds was amusing to Bishop. But, after nearly three days, the sideshow had become tedious and unpleasant, even for the low-key and difficult-to-ruffle Bishop.

A Christmas luncheon hosted by Cason Kellis at a local sports bar earlier that day—Friday, December 20—had served to light the fuse of the personality conflict between Nelson and Wilmeth. Kellis had arranged and paid for the luncheon for the entire audit team, including Paula Henderson and John Kelly. Also in attendance was Karol Eliason, the Kellis clone who was serving as the concurring partner on the BRIC audit engagement.

Near the end of the luncheon that was held in a small private room of the raucous sports bar, Kellis announced that he had Christmas gifts for every member of the BRIC audit team. Kellis called each member of the team to the front of the room and then gave the auditor his or her gag gift. When it was time to give Nelson and Bishop their gifts, he asked them to come to the front of the room together. The gag gift for each of the audit seniors proved to be what Kellis referred to as a GWR—green wavy ruler. The rulers were made of some synthetic rubber-like material mixed with shredded dollar bills, thus the green color. Kellis, who was in high spirits and obviously enjoying his role as the exuberant emcee of the party, reminded Nelson and Bishop that he had previously warned them that they would need a rubber ruler when auditing BRIC's year-end accruals.

As Kellis handed Nelson her ruler, he placed his arm around her shoulder and whispered something into her ear. Almost immediately, Nelson's blemish-free porcelain complexion began to glow like a red traffic light, which caused Bishop to wonder exactly what Kellis had said to her. He didn't have to wonder long.

Several hours later in the BRIC audit conference room, Jim Wilmeth, a master of snide remarks and double entendres, said "Spank me very much" after Nelson handed him an audit work paper file that he had requested.

A startled Nelson immediately snapped at Wilmeth, "Just where did that come from?"

Wilmeth laughed before responding. "You think I don't know what Kellis whispered in your ear at lunch today? Come on, Blondie. He's used that same line before with other cute subordinates."

"Listen! A partner can get away with those kinds of wisecracks, but don't think you can, Buster!"

"Oh, I'm so scared, Miss Prim and Proper. What are you going to do? Report me on the firm hotline?"

The hotline referred to by Wilmeth was a telephone number that firm employees could call to anonymously report job-related complaints or suggestions of any type.

After Wilmeth left for a meeting at his downtown office, Nelson told Bishop that she didn't appreciate Wilmeth's crude and often sexist remarks. Although Bishop liked Wilmeth and identified with him, he realized that the audit manager often crossed the line when interacting with Nelson.

After several moments passed, Bishop responded to Nelson's statement. "Yeah, I agree. Jim is often out of line with you. Hopefully, since we are going to be working together for a while, he will be more professional in the future."

Nelson had seemed surprised, pleasantly surprised, by Bishop's supportive statements. A few minutes later as she was preparing to leave the conference room for the night, she turned to Bishop and asked him if he would like to share a pizza with her at Curcio's, a nearby pizzeria.

"Sure," he replied quickly.

Bishop didn't want to become close friends with Nelson, or Wilmeth, for that matter, but he thought it was harmless for him to go out with her for a pizza. Besides, it meant he didn't have to throw another frozen dinner in his microwave when he returned to his apartment.

The unexpected pizza date with Emma Nelson went well. The two auditors shared several laughs, one at the expense of Jim Wilmeth's habit of wearing ties that clashed horribly with his business suits. Bishop was glad that his relationship with Nelson had improved over the past couple of months. But he also recognized that staying on good terms with both Nelson and Wilmeth would require him to tread lightly when the inevitable dust-ups occurred between the two of them.

As he made the short drive to his apartment after saying goodbye to Emma Nelson, Michael Bishop realized that everyone else was preparing for Christmas. Cason Kellis had instructed the BRIC audit team to take off both Christmas Eve and Christmas Day, which were Tuesday and Wednesday of the following week. Unlike his coworkers, Bishop wasn't looking forward to the brief Christmas vacation. Because his mother and sister lived in the small city of Seal Beach, California, 25 miles south of downtown Los Angeles, it wasn't possible for him to spend the holiday with them. Instead, Bishop planned to fill his fridge with frozen dinners and soft drinks and spend his two-day respite from the BRIC audit conference room watching one movie after another on Netflix.

An hour later, while Bishop was lying on his bed watching the final few minutes of an NBA game, a text message arrived on his phone. The text message was from his former wife, Brooke: "Nothing serious. Please give me a call tomorrow."

Brooke, a physical therapist, also lived in southern California. Michael and Brooke had dated throughout high school. Their relationship continued when they both enrolled in California State University, Long Beach. Three years later, they married when Brooke was two months pregnant. Their son, John Oliver Bishop, was born December 21. When he was ten months old, Ollie, a happy and healthy baby who was already walking, died unexpectedly and tragically from sudden infant death syndrome.

Following their son's death, Brooke tried to persuade Michael to attend meetings of a grief support group with her—the group was for parents who had lost children. Michael couldn't or wouldn't go with Brooke to the meetings. The last thing he wanted to do was to talk about his son's death or commiserate with other grieving parents who were complete strangers. In looking back, that had been the first crack in their relationship. Eighteen months later, that crack had widened into a chasm and Brooke filed for divorce.

Michael dropped out of college and began driving a delivery truck for a local furniture store following the death of his son. Because of his mother's insistence, he later returned to school and completed a five-year accounting degree. He accepted a job with a Big Four accounting firm that allowed him to work for one of its large Midwestern offices. It wasn't that he wanted to get away from his mother and sister, or Brooke; he just wanted to get away, period.

To his knowledge, no one in his office, including the individuals he had worked with most closely, knew of either Ollie or Brooke. He would never consider telling anyone about either of them. His past was his business and no one else's. Plus, he didn't need or want anyone's pity.

Michael realized that he sometimes became depressed. The blues arrived like clockwork on certain dates, most notably Ollie's birthday, Christmas Day, and the day he passed away. On a couple of occasions, Michael had considered seeing a therapist. But, after a day or two, his depression subsided and he resumed his life, as best he could.

Before saying goodnight to Ollie, Michael made a mental note to call Brooke the following afternoon. As he turned off the lamp, he hoped that he would go to sleep quickly since midnight was only 45 minutes away. If he wasn't asleep by then, he knew that it would be a very long night for him.

Chapter 8

Monday, December 23

Ten minutes before noon, almost time for lunch, and was Michael Bishop ever ready for a break. If one more person in BRIC's corporate offices wished him "Merry Christmas," he wasn't sure that he could respond in kind. Christmas was something to be endured rather than enjoyed for Bishop. He didn't resent others enjoying Christmas; he just wished that they wouldn't impose their happiness on him.

Jim Wilmeth had told the members of the BRIC audit team that they could leave at 5 p.m., but Bishop had invented a reason to stay a while later. He had told Wilmeth that he would lock up and make sure that everything was secure for the two-day Christmas break.

The minimum degree of security that his firm provided for audit work papers amazed Bishop. Bishop knew that if they were intent on doing so, Bud Wallace or other client personnel could easily gain access to the auditors' workspaces. Once the locked trunk in the audit conference room was breached, the saboteurs would have direct access to some of the most important documents for the BRIC engagement since hard copies of the audit program, audit checklists, and several audit planning memos had been printed and placed in that trunk. With a little more effort, they could hack into all of the electronic work paper files on the laptop computers inside the trunk.

Auditors lectured their clients concerning the importance of controls, but they didn't take those lectures to heart when it came to their own operations. There was no doubt in Bishop's mind that many ethically-challenged clients had taken advantage of security lapses by their independent auditors.

After his colleagues left at 5 p.m., Bishop intended to stay busy by drafting outlines of the summary work paper memos that would be needed for the accounts that were his responsibility. He wouldn't finalize those memos for several weeks, but, given the extraordinary nature of the BRIC audit engagement, he wanted to be sure that the work papers he prepared, particularly his summary memos, were precise and flawless in terms of their logical structure, accuracy, references to relevant professional standards, and, most importantly, their overall conclusions. He realized that there was a wide range of possible outcomes to the BRIC debacle in which he was now trapped. In five years, he might very well be sitting in a packed federal courtroom explaining the details of a BRIC audit work paper that he had prepared to a squad of nitpicking, flesh-eating attorneys and twelve mildly attentive civilians who didn't know a debit from a credit.

As he was outlining his summary memos, Bishop paused to write a brief note in a personal file that he maintained on his laptop computer. The note reminded Bishop to research his firm's "dissociation" policy. If worse came to worse, Bishop would consider dissociating himself from questionable decisions made by his superiors for the accounts on which he had spent considerable time. As he wrote that note, the thought occurred to Bishop that every audit should be performed as if a group of rabid and self-interested third parties would be combing through the work papers in minute detail searching for gaffes, blunders, and even minor omissions and oversights in the audit procedures that had been applied.

Earlier that afternoon, Bud Wallace had stopped by to speak with Bishop as he worked in the audit conference room. Because Wilmeth and Nelson were there, Wallace asked Bishop to come by his office later when he reached a stopping point in his work. After Wallace left, Wilmeth asked what secrets Bishop and the accounting manager were keeping from the rest of the audit team.

The innocent quip unsettled Bishop briefly. After a few moments passed, he responded by telling Wilmeth that Wallace had asked to review and approve the materiality thresholds for each of BRIC's key accounts. Bishop's witty retort prompted a disapproving glance from Nelson and elicited an "Oh, is that all" rejoinder from Wilmeth. At the time, Bishop made a mental note to tell Wallace to be more cautious in the future.

An hour or so later, Bishop went to Wallace's office. Wallace told Bishop that he would come by the audit conference room at 7:45 p.m. and take him to an unused office on the seventh floor where their meeting would take place. As Bishop was returning to the conference room, he considered the possibility that he should be concerned about his personal safety, but then he quickly dismissed the thought. In his mind, the worst that could happen to him wasn't all that serious.

A few minutes before 8 p.m., Wallace and Bishop stopped outside a small office on the seventh floor of the BRIC headquarters building. After Wallace unlocked the door, Bishop stepped inside; Wallace followed and then closed the door behind him. Seated on the far side of the room were two men neither of whom was a BRIC divisional controller. The men were wearing charcoal business suits, white button-down shirts, paisley ties, and wing tipped shoes.

Wallace first introduced Bishop to "Charles" and then to "Zed." Wallace told Bishop that the two men were attorneys that he and the four divisional controllers had retained. The attorneys, who were in their mid-thirties, reminded Bishop of prototype young audit partners with his firm: they were physically fit, square-jawed, impeccably attired, and "all business." Ironically, each of them was better suited to serve as a prototype of the typical young audit partner of a Big Four firm than the flippant, bow-tied, and hyperkinetic Cason Kellis.

After Wallace and Bishop seated themselves in chairs that faced the two men, Wallace began to speak. Before he had finished his first sentence, Bishop interrupted him.

"Excuse me, but could I see your business cards, please?" Bishop calmly asked Charles and Zed.

After several moments of silence, Charles responded. "At this point, Mr. Bishop, I would prefer that we not exchange personal information."

Wallace glanced at Bishop momentarily and then began speaking again.

Once more, Bishop interrupted him. "So, the way it works is that you know me, but I have no idea who the two of you are?"

For a few moments, both attorneys sat stone-faced not reacting to Bishop's question. Finally, Charles spoke—during the entire meeting Zed was destined to not speak a word. "Michael. I understand your point of view. Completely." After a brief pause, he continued. "Maybe we can compromise. We will let you see our business cards, but we would like for you to return them."

Bishop sat silently but nodded his head in agreement. Charles and then Zed handed their business cards to him. Bishop studied the business cards for several moments. In fact, there was not much to study, other than the name of each man—"Charles E. Payne" and "Zedekiah C. Morris," the designation "Attorney at Law," and a local address that was simply a post office box number.

After Bishop returned the business cards to the two men, Wallace looked at Bishop, waiting for an indication that it was okay for him to proceed. When Bishop gave no such signal, Wallace began speaking once more.

Wallace explained that when he asked Bishop to meet with him, he had intended to have two of the divisional controllers present. But then, after discussing the matter with Charles and Zed, the attorneys had decided that it would be best for them to be present rather than the divisional controllers.

The two attorneys had told Wallace that the "creative accounting" he and the divisional controllers had been applying for BRIC Industries qualified as "fraud" and violated multiple provisions of the federal securities laws. The attorneys had also told Wallace that neither the federal courts nor the SEC would accept a "good soldier" defense in such circumstances. Although Suzanne Jennings had insisted that the fraudulent misrepresentations be entered in the company's accounting records, Wallace and his four subordinates were personally responsible for agreeing to do so.

Next, Wallace told Bishop that he and the divisional controllers did not want to go to jail and hoped to avoid being sanctioned by the SEC or any other regulatory body. Wallace said that the reason he had asked Bishop to meet with him this evening was to explain a plan that he had conceived. If this plan proved to be successful, he and the divisional controllers hoped that they would "escape" from the "nightmare" in which they were trapped by losing nothing more than their jobs. If they could somehow avoid drawing the attention of the state board of accountancy, they believed they could retain their CPA certificates and continue their careers in accounting.

"That night when we met in the Grotto, I obviously had too much to drink and wound up telling you way too much," Wallace said after he turned to his right to speak directly to Bishop. "I intended to speak to you much later in the audit, but my, uh … uh, indiscretion forced my hand. And so, I decided that I had to speak to you much sooner."

Wallace then told Bishop that the rumor that a large private equity firm was planning to extend an offer to purchase BRIC Industries was true. Suzanne Jennings had suggested that the offer would likely be made within two weeks after BRIC filed its 10-K in late February.

"Michael, we realize that we have to end this accounting fraud before that happens. If we don't, then after the buyout there's a very real likelihood that the owners of the private equity firm will figure out that we tampered with BRIC's books. That discovery would trigger accusations that would likely result in an SEC investigation, multiple lawsuits, and ultimately the filing of criminal charges against each one of us." Wallace paused as he briefly shook his head. "Jennings lives in some alternate universe and insists that won't happen, that we can dupe the private equity firm's accountants just like we duped you guys, the auditors. The fact of the matter is, I think that if the fraud is uncovered, Jennings plans to blame it all on me and the divisional controllers. She's been extremely careful to avoid leaving any trail of incriminating evidence that leads back to her. The only person she ever directly discusses the accounting manipulations with is me and there are never any notes or written instructions to document what she tells me to do."

Wallace leaned forward and clasped his hands together.

"Jennings insisted from the beginning that this 'earnings management' strategy, as she calls it, was only temporary. Because the turnaround plan that she, Hakes, and Zimmer were implementing would eventually improve the company's operating results, she assured me repeatedly that we would eventually 'cleanse' the accounting records of the bogus amounts that she convinced me to book. But that has never happened. Every quarter it has been necessary to do more and more crazy stuff to manufacture the earnings numbers that her and her two buddies want to report in BRIC's SEC filings."

Wallace explained that his plan to end the fraud would involve "accidentally" providing information to the auditors that revealed the large overstatement of BRIC's year-end inventory. He would give that information to the auditors a few days before BRIC's earnings announcement that was scheduled for February 24.

"Inventory is the 'go to' account for Jennings," Wallace explained. "Although every key revenue and expense number is fudged, when we are still short at the end of a quarter, Jennings typically tells me to inflate inventory somehow to reduce cost of goods sold. There is no doubt that she will tell me to ratchet up the inventory numbers at the end of this year's fourth quarter. And by a lot."

Wallace continued with a remorseful tone to his voice. "In the past, we have pulled off all sorts of charades to inflate inventory. We have created bogus in-transit inventory at year-end, included consigned inventory owned by other parties in our inventory counts, overstated the per unit purchase prices of raw material components, and created fictitious inventory. Believe it or not, we 'store' the phony inventory in a virtual warehouse that is accounted for in a subsidiary ledger that you guys don't know about." Wallace paused briefly as he shook his head. "We have even hired outside moving companies to transfer high-priced inventory components between warehouses overnight during the final few days of the year when we take our physical inventory counts. That serves to both overstate inventory and to trick the auditors—your guys—into test counting the same inventory twice. Of course, that trick only works because the auditors from your firm have always told us which inventory sites they are going to test count."

Wallace told Bishop that he had come up with several possible strategies for "accidentally" giving auditors access to information that documented the year-end inventory overstatement. The easiest strategy to implement would be revealing the existence of Warehouse 99—where the fictitious inventory was "stored." But, according to Wallace, that would set off "all sorts of fire alarms" and cast doubt on the integrity of all BRIC's accounting records. What he hoped to do was develop a strategy that would allow him to argue credibly to the auditors that the given inventory overstatements were the result of accounting "errors" rather than fraud.

Over the next few weeks, Wallace would settle on a plan of action for revealing the inventory overstatement to Bishop and his fellow auditors and then begin working on the details to implement it.

"Regardless of how we decide to burst the bubble, so to speak, the collective inventory misstatement is going to be so large that Cason Kellis won't be able to simply ignore it," Wallace said emphatically as he glanced at the two attorneys. "At that point, I plan to go to Jennings and tell her that this has to end. I am going to tell her that it doesn't make any sense to continue this accounting sham and that myself and the divisional controllers aren't going to do her dirty work anymore. I am going to tell her that in addition to announcing the big earnings miss for the fourth quarter in the year-end earnings press release, she also has to disclose that the company expects a poor first quarter. I could then hide a lot, if not most, of the remaining fraudulent misstatements in first-quarter write-offs. The bad fourth-quarter numbers and the disclosure of the expected poor operating results for the first quarter will send BRIC's stock price into a tailspin and almost certainly cause the private equity firm to cancel its buyout plan."

For several moments, Wallace sat silently as he nervously wrung his hands. "Hopefully, none of this will trigger an SEC investigation ... or any stockholder lawsuits," he said as his voice began to crack. "If it works out as planned, then we may be able to escape with our necks. Of course, we realize that we will be canned at the first opportunity unless the board of directors fires Hakes, Zimmer, and Jennings first."

Wallace gazed at the two expressionless, emotionless attorneys before continuing. "I may just be whistling in the wind here. I mean ... I don't really know how all of this is going to play out. But, regardless, at least this plan gives us some hope. If I just try to force Jennings' hand now and tell her that I'm going to report the fraud to the SEC, then we are pretty much dead in the water. We will be tarred and feathered by the SEC, lose our certificates, and be forced to peddle insurance or aluminum siding from door to door."

Wallace paused to muster the energy to continue. "Like I said the other night, Kellis seems to the kind of guy who might roll over when a client places pressure on him. I don't think that he will try to look the other way when he sees how much BRIC's inventory is overstated. But ... you never know."

Following an extended silence, Wallace began his plea for Bishop's cooperation.

"Michael, all that I am asking from you is that you do your job. If it appears that Kellis is dragging his feet or is somehow working with Jennings to continue distorting BRIC's operating results, you could nudge him in the right direction. Or if you don't feel comfortable doing that, at least come to me and let me know what is going on."

Wallace stopped and spent several moments staring at the floor.

"Then, maybe ... maybe ... I could do something to force Jennings' hand. But, again, that shouldn't be necessary if you will just do your job, Michael," he said passionately. "You're an audit senior and they have to listen to you. You could even go to Eliason, the concurring partner, and tell him that Kellis is refusing to do the right thing. That guy won't have much of a vested interest in the audit and so he may be willing to blow the whistle. Or you could call your firm's anonymous hotline, or whatever you call it, and report the fact that Kellis is rolling over and becoming complicit in a client fraud."

Moments later, Wallace added as an afterthought, "Of course, I'm also asking that you not ... uh ... uh ... blow the whistle on us prematurely, I mean, over the next couple of months. That you let this all play out until the end of the audit when we implement our plan."

When Wallace completed his sales pitch to gain Bishop's cooperation, a tense silence fell over the small room. Throughout Wallace's monologue, Charles and Zed had sat staring at Bishop. It seemed to Bishop that they were trying to gauge his every reaction to each word that Wallace spoke. Bishop occasionally glanced at them but mostly focused his attention on the closed window shades behind them as he sat immobile, passively but keenly listening to Wallace.

Bishop wasn't familiar with the ethical responsibilities of attorneys, but he doubted that top-notch attorneys would allow a client to continue engaging in criminal activity. Plus, Bishop suspected that most attorneys would refuse to be present when a client discussed an ongoing criminal enterprise with an independent third party. The relevant phrase in this context he believed was "officer of the court." Although Bishop wasn't sure exactly what that phrase meant, he believed it referred to the fact that attorneys, similar to independent auditors, have an obligation to act with integrity and in the public interest at all times.

Despite the suspicious presence of the two attorneys, the story told by Wallace was both plausible and compelling to Bishop. He had witnessed firsthand the overbearing demeanor of Suzanne Jennings. In a few minutes time during the earlier audit planning meeting, she had crushed any morsels of self-respect and professional dignity that Cason Kellis might have possessed before the meeting. It was certainly reasonable to believe that she had browbeaten Wallace into misrepresenting BRIC's financial statements.

———

Finally, Bishop broke the silence by asking, "What if I don't go along with this?" As he asked the question, Bishop stared at Charles who didn't change his facial expression or otherwise react to the question.

"If that is your decision, then, well, that's it. I mean, you are obviously free to do whatever you think is appropriate," Wallace replied softly. "You certainly don't owe us anything. I understand that I have imposed on you tremendously by sharing this information with you in the first place."

After a brief pause, Wallace decided to make one more bid for Bishop's cooperation.

"I would just like to say that the five of us are not bad guys. If you got to know us, I think you would find that we are just normal, everyday accountants who work nine to five. More like eight to seven, actually."

Wallace tried to laugh at his frail attempt at humor, but the forced chuckle caught in his throat and he passed it off as a cough.

"I'm divorced, thanks to my drinking problem and the fact that I work too much. But the other four guys, the four divisional controllers, are early in their professional careers and are family men. Each one of them has small children at home." Wallace paused. When he resumed, he was speaking almost in a whisper. "I would respectfully ask that, or hope that, you would at least consider the impact that all of this might have on those innocent children, and their mothers, before you decide what you will do."

Wallace's reference to the "innocent children" had the desired impact on Bishop. For the first time, he allowed his emotions to surface. He shook his head wearily and then turned and stared at the blank wall to his right.

"By the way," Wallace said, "I want you to know that no one will ever know, no one outside the four of us, will ever know about this meeting. The divisional controllers don't know that I spoke to you about this in the Grotto that evening or that I am speaking to you now. The only thing they know is that we have all agreed to end this fraud and that I will take the lead in pressing Jennings to accept a disappointing earnings report for the fourth quarter. They have also all agreed that I will be the one who deals with the attorneys we have hired." Wallace placed his right hand on the back of Bishop's chair to emphasize the point he was about to make. "I promise you that once we leave here tonight, it will be as if this meeting never took place. Whatever happens, and who knows what may happen, no one else will ever know that we met." After a few moments, Wallace added forcefully, "No one."

For several minutes, Bishop sat silently deep in thought, considering his options. Again, he admitted to himself that Wallace's presentation had been very convincing. Wallace and the four divisional controllers had stepped out onto a slippery slope by making a bad decision. More bad decisions had followed. At some point, they had awakened to the stone cold and frightening reality that they were mired in a quagmire, a large-scale accounting fraud. They had been conned into becoming active participants in that fraud by their self-serving, overbearing white-collar bosses. Bishop realized that it was a common storyline, an all-too-common storyline in the get-rich age of executive stock options, huge year-end bonuses linked to reported earnings, and the enormous pressure exerted on public companies by Wall Street to meet or exceed their consensus earnings forecasts each quarterly reporting period.

Bishop didn't relish the idea of becoming a member of a criminal conspiracy, even a passive member. And he certainly didn't look forward to the task of keeping a lid on BRIC's accounting fraud for the next two months. Then again, two months wouldn't make much of a difference, he reasoned. Once more, he thought of the four divisional controllers who were, at most, just a few years older than himself. Then, he thought of their children. Small children who would soon be gathering around the family Christmas tree to rip open presents left by Santa. At that moment, he made his decision.

Before revealing his decision, there was an issue that Bishop wanted to raise, an issue that would allow him to put the haughty and self-important attorneys on the spot.

"I have a question," Bishop said as he stared directly into Charles' steel gray eyes. "It seems to me that this information that we are sitting on, that you want me to sit on, is very valuable inside information that could be used to make a quick profit in the stock market. Does that pose a problem for me?"

Without hesitating, Charles responded, "Mr. Bishop, I am not your attorney and I am not going to address any legal issues with you."

Not pleased by his inability to pry any meaningful information from Charles, Bishop shook his head in frustration and then shifted his gaze away from the attorney.

After another extended silence, Wallace spoke. "Well, I guess that we are done here." He then added with a forced smile, "I don't want to delay the start of that huge two-day Christmas holiday that you have to look forward to."

Bishop glanced at Wallace. The accounting manager appeared to be emotionally and physically drained. It was also obvious that, although he was desperate to know, he wasn't going to ask Bishop what his decision was.

After turning away from Wallace, Bishop slowly got to his feet and then took two steps toward the office door. As he placed his right hand on the doorknob, be turned back toward Wallace. "This solution, or whatever you want to call it, sounds reasonable to me. I won't mention this to anyone during the next two months. And there is no reason for you and me to ever discuss this again."

Wallace stood and faced Bishop. "I understand. I understand completely, Michael. I won't in any way refer, directly or indirectly, to any of this with you over the next two months. You have my word."

As Bishop stepped through the doorway of the office on his way out, Wallace said "Merry Christmas" to him in a voice choked with emotion.

Bishop winced inwardly as he paused. He glanced back at Wallace once more and briefly nodded before walking away.

Chapter 9

Tuesday, December 31

4:30 A.M.

The shrill and annoying bursts startled Michael Bishop. After rolling over and turning off his alarm clock, he laid in his bed for several moments and wondered why he had set the alarm for 4:30 a.m. As the cobwebs in his brain faded away, Bishop remembered what day it was: New Year's Eve.

New Year's Eve is a busy day for independent auditors, at least those employed by the Big Four accounting firms. The majority of Big Four audit clients have fiscal years that coincide with the calendar year. Those clients involved in manufacturing, wholesaling, and retailing industries commonly take physical inventories during the final few days of the year, with December 31 easily being the most popular day for that tedious task. To confirm the existence assertion and to gather evidence relevant to other management assertions for the important inventory account, independent auditors observe the taking of the physical inventory, do test counts of their own, and collect other audit evidence at their clients' inventory sites.

Most members of the audit staff of Bishop's practice office below the rank of audit manager had at least one inventory observation assignment on New Year's Eve. Because of those assignments, Jim Wilmeth had jokingly told his subordinates that they could have the day off, meaning that they didn't have to show up at BRIC Industries' headquarters before or after their inventory observation. For most members of the BRIC audit team that meant a relatively short work day of six hours or less on New Year's Eve. Wilmeth had also told the BRIC audit team members that they didn't have to show up for work until 1 p.m. on New Year's Day.

New Year's Eve wouldn't be a short day for Michael Bishop. Initially, he had been given two relatively simple inventory observation assignments both of which involved public warehouses. Those warehouses were within a short distance of each other on the metroplex's far eastern perimeter, more than 20 miles from his apartment complex. The inventory-taking procedures at the two warehouses, which had common ownership, were scheduled to begin at 6 a.m. and were expected to be completed by noon.

Emma Nelson had been given a "plum" inventory assignment involving an orthopedic hospital operated by a religious order. Adjacent to the orthopedic hospital was a small warehouse that served as a storage unit for prostheses. The physical inventory at that site was scheduled to begin at 1 p.m. and, according to a representative of the religious order, "would require no more than two hours to complete."

Nelson had mentioned over lunch the previous day that she planned to be in the BRIC audit conference room both before and after her brief inventory observation assignment so that she could take advantage of the "peace and quiet" and catch up on some of her work. At that point, Bishop had offered to do the inventory observation for her since the orthopedic hospital was less than one mile from the public warehouses that he would be visiting. Nelson accepted Bishop's thoughtful offer. She said she would contact the audit manager who was responsible for the audit of the religious order and ask her to forward Bishop a copy of the inventory observation audit program. Later that evening, the audit manager emailed Bishop and told him that she hadn't prepared an audit program for the inventory observation. She told Bishop that it would be sufficient for him to observe the counting procedures, take some inventory test counts, and obtain copies of the instructions given to the count teams.

At five p.m. on Monday afternoon, December 30, Cason Kellis had called Emma Nelson while she was working in the audit conference room. The audit partner had just received a call from a fellow audit partner in the firm's Philadelphia practice office. That partner desperately needed someone in Kellis's office to observe the taking of inventory at a large department store on the near northeast edge of the metroplex. The inventory counting wouldn't begin until 30 minutes or so after the store closed at 6 p.m. on New Year's Eve. Kellis told Nelson that because he owed his fellow partner a huge favor, he wanted her to choose a rookie staff accountant on the BRIC audit team who would be available at 6:30 p.m. to do the inventory observation at the retail store.

After she hung up the phone, Nelson told Bishop of the bad news that she would be forced to deliver to one of the rookies on their audit team. Nelson was aware that the four rookies were planning to attend a New Year's Eve party for their start class that was being sponsored by the practice office.

"Hey, I'm going to be spending my entire day over on the east side," Bishop told Nelson. "That store should be within twenty minutes of the orthopedic hospital. I can eat dinner after finishing the hospital job and then drive over there. A big department store like that should be well prepared for taking the year-end inventory, so I should be able to knock out the assignment in a few hours."

"Come on, Michael, you already have a full day booked. There's no need to take on this job as well," Nelson replied.

"I really don't mind, Emma. I don't have anything planned for New Year's Eve. No reason to ruin the big party for one of the rookies."

Nelson hesitated before responding. Her facial expression signaled that she was surprised that her handsome colleague didn't have anything planned for New Year's Eve. To that point, she still had no idea of his relationship status, but the fact that he had no plans for New Year's Eve suggested that Bishop was definitely unattached. After a few moments, she replied, "Well, okay," and said that she would email Kellis and have him forward Bishop the inventory observation program for the department store.

Ironically, none of the inventory observations that Bishop would be completing involved BRIC Industries, which had two major inventory sites on the outskirts of the metroplex. The physical inventory at one of those sites would be observed by Jackson Coleman, while the other would be observed by Becky Linton. Coleman and Linton would each be assisted by a rookie staff accountant on the BRIC audit team.

Given what he had been told by Bud Wallace, Bishop was more than happy to avoid the year-end physical inventory observations for the two BRIC sites. In fact, he was hoping that the BRIC inventory work papers would be totally devoid of his name.

———————

After taking a shower, pulling on a pair of blue jeans, a t-shirt, and a warm hoodie, Michael Bishop rushed out the door at 5:00 a.m. to make the long drive to the east side of the metroplex where the two public warehouses were located. On the way, he stopped at a McDonald's to grab a morning meal of two Egg Mc-Muffins and a large orange juice.

At the site of the first warehouse, Bishop introduced himself to the warehouse manager and told him that he would be observing the physical inventory. Bishop then walked the 100 yards to the other warehouse and did the same.

Over the past three years, Bishop had observed the taking of the physical inventory at several public warehouses. Although the nature of the specific tasks that had to be performed varied depending upon the type of inventory being stored, it was typically an easy assignment because most public warehouses hire an outside firm to count their inventory. Professional inventory counters are generally well organized and very efficient, which reduces the number of test counts that auditors must take.

After meeting the two warehouse managers, Bishop reviewed the copies of the physical inventory instructions that they had given him. He then toured the first warehouse to familiarize himself with its physical layout and the types of inventory stored in each of its sections. Next, he spent an hour taking and recording inventory test counts at that warehouse and then two additional hours observing the inventory count teams. While observing the count teams, he occasionally took notes. Those notes documented the measures taken to ensure that all inventory was counted once and only once, any evidence of damaged inventory, and the presence of any inventory that had been segregated for some purpose, such as inventory that was being prepared for shipment. Bishop then walked to the second warehouse and repeated the same procedures for that facility.

For each warehouse, Bishop also obtained the documents that the inventory suborder audit program required him to request from the warehouse manager — "suborder" meant the inventory observation was being completed for another practice office that had the responsibility for preparing the audit program for the job. The documents he obtained included, among others, copies of the insurance policies for each warehouse and copies of recent inspection reports prepared by the local fire department for the warehouses.

1:05 P.M.

Because the manager of the second warehouse spent considerable time searching for its most recent fire department inspection report, Bishop was behind schedule when he pulled out of the facility's parking lot at 12:45 p.m. Lunch consisted of a bean burrito, a taco, and a giant-sized Diet Pepsi that he ordered at the drive-by window of a Taco Bell on his way to the orthopedic hospital.

Bishop arrived at the hospital five minutes after 1 p.m. but spent another five minutes inhaling his bean burrito as he sat in his car. By the time he found his way inside the orthopedic hospital's warehouse, the counting had already begun.

The interior of the small warehouse was littered with large steel tables, multi-layered storage shelves, and stacks of different-sized boxes, many of which were overflowing with inventory items. Unlike the public warehouses, the count teams for the orthopedic warehouse appeared to have no prior inventory-taking experience. It was also readily apparent that the count teams were not happy to be spending a portion of New Year's Eve rummaging around the musty, windowless storage facility — Bishop later learned that each year the hospital assigned the inventory counting task to "new hires" from its janitorial and maintenance departments.

After just a few moments spent observing the count teams, Bishop realized that they weren't using preformatted count sheets. Instead, the teams were recording their counts on blank pieces of white paper. And, although they were working in groups of two, the twosomes were not count "teams" — each individual was counting and recording. Bishop also noticed that there was no rhyme or reason to the counting procedures. The individuals seemed to be picking tables, shelves, and boxes at random to count. Making matters worse, the prosthetic arms, legs, and other items that Bishop didn't recognize were stored haphazardly without the benefit of any organizational scheme.

Bishop approached a young lady with purple hair and asked who was supervising the counting procedures.

"I dunno," the young lady responded glumly as she dug into a large box of what appeared to be broken prosthetic legs.

"Excuse me," Bishop said as he tapped Purple Hair's partner on the shoulder. "Can you tell me where your supervisor is?"

"He's probably home asleep, which is where I should be," the angry young man snapped as he adjusted his sunglasses.

"Well, who is supervising the counting?" Bishop asked. When the young man didn't respond, Bishop decided to go vernacular. "Uh, who's running the show here?"

The young man tilted his head forward and peered at Bishop over his sunglasses. "S'posed to be some dude here from a arditering company." After a brief pause, the young man asked, "Are you the dude?"

After halting the counting, Bishop spent a few minutes formatting an improvised inventory count sheet and then 20 minutes trying to find a copier to make multiple copies of the count sheet. When he returned to the warehouse, only 2.5 counting teams were still there.

For the next two hours, Bishop and his helpers organized the inventory by device and size. He identified five categories of devices, the final one being "Other," and three size classes—small, medium, and large. Broken items were segregated in one corner of the warehouse.

The actual counting began at 3:40 p.m; at exactly 6:05 p.m., the counting was completed. Bishop thanked the three counters still left at that point, put a large rubber band around the count sheets, and rushed to his car.

6:55 P.M.

Because of a wreck on a freeway, Bishop was forced to navigate his way through residential neighborhoods filled with narrow, winding streets and cul-de-sacs as he tried to locate the department store that was the site of his final assignment of the day. When he arrived at a few minutes before 7 p.m., he was surprised to find the store's parking lot two-thirds full. After making his way inside the store and tracking down the store manager, Bishop was told that the store would close at 9 p.m. and the inventory counting was scheduled to begin at 10 p.m.

"But the information I got was that the store closed at six p.m. and that the counting would begin no later than six-thirty."

"Sorry, Bro. Don't know who told you that," the manager responded over his shoulder after turning away to assist a customer who was searching for the cosmetics department.

The inventory counting began at 10:45 p.m. Fifteen minutes later, an electrical malfunction caused the store to go pitch black. The store's auxiliary lights came on after 90 seconds or so and provided just enough illumination for Bishop to see his right hand when he fully extended his arm. Forty minutes passed before the store's maintenance staff was successful in hooking up a borrowed generator and getting the store fully illuminated with the exception of the men's apparel department. For the next four hours, that department was an otherworldly domain thanks to a strobe light effect caused by some remaining electrical problem. Not surprisingly, none of the test counts that Bishop performed were in the Twilight Zone.

At the stroke of midnight, the New Year was welcomed by an earsplitting version of *Auld Lang Syne* that was blasted over the store's intercom system. At the time, Bishop happened to be test counting the housewares department. Although he was well aware that smooching client employees might threaten his perceived independence, Bishop couldn't turn down the two grandmotherly types who were counting pots and pans when they asked him for a New Year's kiss.

3:35 A.M.

After organizing his test count sheets and making sure that he had obtained copies of all the required documents, Bishop walked out of the department store at 3:35 a.m. Exhausted, thirsty, and hungry, Bishop stopped at a Dunkin Donuts on the way home—he had eaten dinner eight hours earlier at a Jack in the Box across the street from the department store. For 25 minutes, he sat at the counter of the donut shop enjoying a hot cup of chocolate, two coconut donuts with rainbow sprinkles, and an on-again, off-again conversation with a lonely, gray-haired widow named Patricia—"my friends call me Patty"—from Poughkeepsie, New York, whose personal space he had apparently invaded after sitting five stools and more than 15 feet to her right in the otherwise deserted donut shop. On the way out of the shop, Bishop wished Patty a Happy New Year and surprised her with a quick peck on the cheek. "Oh my, who knew that I would find love tonight at Dunkin Donuts," Patty remarked after returning the favor to Bishop.

4:25 A.M.

Bishop made his way gingerly up the stairs to his third-floor apartment, gripping the handrail all the way, while trying to avoid slipping on the cat-gut slick stairs that were glazed with ice thanks to a winter storm that had blown in from the north as he sat discussing Lady Gaga, teenage pregnancy, and immigration reform with the widely read and profoundly opinionated Poughkeepsie Patty.

Moments after ditching his food-stained hoodie and pitching his t-shirt and jeans on the floor, Bishop glanced at his cell phone. It was 4:25 a.m. After saying good night to Ollie and turning off his bedside lamp, Bishop laid down on his bed and pledged that he would never again volunteer to complete a New Year's Eve inventory observation intended for someone else.

Chapter 10

Thursday, January 9

"You may not wrap up the price tests for the raw materials inventory until next Monday or Tuesday? You've got to be kidding me! Last Friday, you told me that you would have those tests done by 'mid-week.' I don't know about you, Jackson, but I took 'mid-week' to mean Wednesday. Of this week. As in yesterday! You have to get those tests done so that you can start on the valuation tests for the WIP and finished goods inventories."

Jackson Coleman took the dressing down from Emma Nelson well, too well, in fact. As he stood next to Nelson who was seated at the audit conference room table, he smiled smugly as he adjusted and then readjusted his thin celery-hued European tie that matched his snug celery-hued European-cut suit.

"So, you think this is not serious? You think it's amusing?"

"Uh, no. I just, uh, didn't know what to say," a wide-eyed and now properly penitent Coleman replied.

Nelson turned to Michael Bishop who was sitting a few feet away to her right at the conference room table, directly across from Jim Wilmeth who was clearly enjoying Nelson's latest tirade directed at one of the staff accountants. "Michael, is there any way that you could spare Kaimee Mongold for a couple of days? I know she is helping you on the long-term debt accounts, but I think it is critical that we wrap up these raw materials price tests as soon as possible. Jackson is finding all sorts of exceptions. Once those tests are completed, someone has to sit down with Bud Wallace and figure out why there are so many mispriced components in the raw materials inventory accounts."

"Sure," Bishop responded. "I will tell Kaimee to find a reasonable stopping point and then she will be free to work with Jackson." Bishop ignored Nelson's reference to Bud Wallace. Over the past two weeks, Nelson had realized that Bishop, like herself, was avoiding Wallace. She hadn't asked why Bishop was avoiding Wallace, most likely because doing so might focus unwanted attention on her own troubled relationship with the general accounting manager.

Kaimee Mongold was one of the four rookie staff accountants who had joined the BRIC audit team in December. Similar to the other rookies, Kaimee was anxious to please but had to be supervised closely. Since the inventory price tests for raw materials were less than challenging—they were mind-numbingly tedious—any rookie accountant could easily perform them. If Bishop had been supervising the fieldwork, he would have requested a rookie "floater" to do the raw materials price tests and immediately put Coleman to work on the more demanding task of testing the per unit values assigned to the work-in-process (WIP) and finished goods inventories.

"Okay, Jackson. It's Thursday morning, January ninth, at eleven-fourteen a.m.," Nelson said after glancing at her pink-faced Franck Muller watch that matched the pale pink, sheer linen blouse she was wearing—Nelson and Coleman shared a penchant for being fashionably stylish. "You can have Kaimee until Saturday evening. That's going to be more than twenty-five chargeable hours. I don't want you to leave here Saturday night until those fricking price tests are done."

Coleman nodded obediently and then slinked away.

Moments later, Jim Wilmeth addressed Nelson. "Whoa, Emmie. Never heard you use a curse word like 'fricking.' Man, I love it when you talk nasty! Spank you very much."

Nelson sprang from her chair, pushed the door of the conference room shut, and then wheeled and faced Wilmeth. "I am warning you, dammit," she said angrily as she waggled her right index finger in Wilmeth's direction. "That's the last 'spanking' comment that I am going to take from you. If you make another one of those cracks, I'm telling Cason Kellis." Before Wilmeth could respond, Nelson snapped, "And quit calling me Emmie or Curls or Blondie. My name is Emmm-uhhh!"

"Hey, Princess, think now. Who originated the 'spanking salon' in the first place? I think it was your best buddy, Captain Kellis, who, the last time I checked, was still in charge of this Good Ship Lollipop." Wilmeth laughed aloud before continuing. "And, by the way, the Captain is not making his normal Friday afternoon curtain call out here, but he's going to show up tomorrow morning. So, you can file your complaint with him in person then."

"Maybe I will just do that," Nelson fired back. "It's good to have an audit partner out here rather than being forced to deal with a career audit manager."

"Yikes, that hurts, Princess. Did you ever consider the possibility that I don't want to be a partner?"

"Like I believe that. Jealousy oozes from your pores every time Cason's around."

"Hmm. Okay, maybe you're right about that," Wilmeth responded before quickly adding, "But at least I get more chicks than Kellis does."

"He's married, you clown."

"Thanks for reinforcing my point," Wilmeth shot back.

It was time for Nelson's next salvo, but instead of responding she grabbed a stack of work papers and marched out of the room.

Bishop, who had purposefully kept his head down during the shouting match, wondered how Nelson and Wilmeth could possibly work together during the tense final weeks of the BRIC audit. During the wrap-up phase of an audit, the supervising senior and audit manager typically spent considerable time one-on-one discussing and clearing review comments made on work papers prepared by their subordinates. Bishop could not imagine Nelson and Wilmeth having even-handed discussions regarding any topic, with the possible exception of how much they disliked each other. Over the past few days, Nelson had been so angry with Wilmeth that she had struggled to be civil to him even when the two of them were in the presence of client personnel.

"Dang, I think I really got under her skin that time," Wilmeth said to Bishop after Nelson left them in her wake. "I wouldn't be surprised if she did say something to Kellis."

Bishop acknowledged Wilmeth's comment with a brief nod of his head as he continued to work.

After several moments had passed, Bishop looked up from his laptop computer and addressed Wilmeth. "You know, Jim. Don't take this the wrong way, but I do think you are being a little rough on Emma. You know, she's under a lot of stress and she's doing the best she can."

Wilmeth was clearly surprised by Bishop's statement. He leaned back in his chair and twirled a pencil between his index finger and thumb before finally responding. "Yeah, you're right on all counts, Michael. I guess I find it hard to draw the line sometimes." Wilmeth's face and voice revealed some modest degree of shame. "Truth is, I only bug her because she is so cute. The only way that a slob like me can get attention from someone like that is to needle her."

Bishop had never heard Wilmeth make self-deprecating comments, but it was obvious to him that the audit manager had an enormous inferiority complex.

After Wilmeth turned his attention back to his computer screen, he quietly said, "Thanks, Michael."

Bishop hoped that Wilmeth would be more professional with Emma Nelson. With seven tension-wracked weeks to go in the audit, Bishop didn't need any more Jerry Springer moments to distract him.

Thankfully, Wilmeth had already announced that beginning the next day he would be spending one week working at the headquarters office of his new hospital client. He planned to return to BRIC headquarters on the morning of January 17. So, for at least a week, Bishop could enjoy some tranquil moments in the audit conference room.

Even when Wilmeth was present at BRIC headquarters, he spent much of his time working on his hospital engagement. In the employee break room one afternoon, Wilmeth had confided in Bishop that he was very interested in the healthcare industry. He had finally been given a healthcare audit assignment after requesting one for years. He told Bishop that he hoped to parlay the knowledge he gained on that audit into a controllership position with a hospital when he was "shown the door" by their employer.

Most of the stress that Emma Nelson faced stemmed from how poorly the BRIC audit was going—just how poorly Nelson wouldn't discover for several weeks to come. The past Friday, Paula Henderson had given Nelson and Bishop a verbal report on the overall condition of BRIC's internal controls. "Lousy" was the term Henderson had used repeatedly in that report. Coming from an alleged internal controls specialist, that was a major indictment of the integrity of BRIC's controls.

Henderson and her team of floating auditors had found excessive exception rates for nearly every internal control test they had performed. Unapproved purchase orders, sales invoices without accompanying shipping advices, missing receiving reports for inventory purchases, improperly classified expenses, and the list went on and on.

John Kelly, who had tested BRIC's data input, processing, and output controls for its major transaction cycles, had also found a litany of problems. While applying a series of tests to BRIC's payroll data, for example, Kelly had discovered several instances in which union employees were not being paid the hourly wage rates mandated by their union contract. Likewise, a software program that computed the payroll tax withholdings for BRIC's hourly employees had not been updated for two months after a new federal law went into effect that impacted those withholdings.

Henderson told Nelson and Bishop that she had never been exposed to a weaker internal control structure. Most troubling to her was the lack of control consciousness exhibited by BRIC's key accounting staff members, including Bud Wallace. According to Henderson, Wallace and his principal subordinates had little or no appreciation for the importance of internal controls.

Because of the deficient internal controls, Henderson didn't believe that she could recommend that an unqualified opinion be issued on BRIC's internal controls over financial reporting. When Bishop asked her what material weaknesses in those controls she had identified, Henderson struggled to come up with specific examples. She finally replied, "Michael, every control is so weak that the only material weakness I would specifically identify would be the material weakness in every control that we tested."

Nelson shielded her face with her left hand as she rolled her eyes at Bishop. When it was apparent that Nelson didn't intend to provide any direction or help to Henderson, Bishop decided that he would.

"Well, Paula, I think that is too general. I think you need to identify more specific or concrete examples of major internal control problems. In fact, if you review the prior year audit work papers, you will find several significant deficiencies in internal controls over financial reporting that were discovered and reported in the summary ICFR memo by last year's audit team." As he spoke, Bishop wondered if Henderson recalled that he had suggested weeks earlier that she access that memo. "If you review those deficiencies, that might give you a starting point for developing a list of significant deficiencies and/or material weaknesses discovered during this year's audit. Just for example, I believe that last year the auditors had a lot of trouble tying the balances of the general ledger controlling accounts for receivables and inventory to the corresponding subsidiary ledgers. Of course, we are finding that same problem this year while performing the substantive tests for those accounts."

Bishop's comment only served to further confound Henderson. "Wait a minute. You mean that I am supposed to check with you and Emma before I draft the ICFR memo and opinion? To find out whether the year-end substantive audit tests have revealed other ICFR problems?"

"Yes," Bishop responded bluntly.

"Oh brother. I wish someone had sat down and explained all of this to me six weeks ago," she replied.

Bishop realized that Henderson had not been properly instructed or supervised. Then again, if she had reviewed the prior year ICFR memo, as he had suggested, she would have had a much better grasp of what was expected of her.

Despite the concerns that Henderson had expressed regarding BRIC's internal controls, the ICFR memo that she subsequently drafted failed to identify any material weaknesses. Instead, her memo discussed the four significant deficiencies in internal control that had been identified in the prior year ICFR memo—her descriptions of those items were taken word for word from that document.

––––––––––

A few minutes after their meeting with Henderson ended, Emma Nelson showed considerable insight, at least in Bishop's opinion, when she asked him point blank, "Do you think this company is even auditable given how terrible the internal controls are?"

"Well, Emma, that's certainly a reasonable question to ask at this point."

"For purposes of the actual financial statement audit, I understand that Cason doesn't plan to place any faith in BRIC's internal controls. But it seems to me that at some point a company's internal controls may be so weak that it is impossible to rely on any number produced by the company's accounting system."

Nelson abruptly shifted the focus of the conversation to an issue of more immediate concern to her.

"Oh, I just thought of something. Michael, have you finished updating the financial ratios spreadsheet for the fourth quarter?"

Bishop had noticed as the audit progressed that one of Nelson's strengths was her ability to focus diligently on the completion of specific audit tasks. On the other hand, she had a limited ability to focus for any extended time on "big picture" issues, such as, the overall "auditability" of a company with wretched internal controls.

"I just finished updating the spreadsheet this morning," Bishop replied. "Granted, if there are any major changes in the year-end working trial balance numbers, I will have to go in and revise the ratios."

Bishop told Nelson that BRIC's profitability ratios for the fourth quarter were remarkably consistent with those for the first three quarters of the year. The ratios that had changed the most during the fourth quarter were the asset management ratios for receivables and inventory. The turnover ratios and corresponding age measures for those two important accounts had worsened considerably during the fourth quarter. BRIC's receivables and inventory turnover ratios for that quarter were less than one-half those of the industry norms.

"The divergence in the profitability and turnover ratios doesn't make sense, right?" Nelson asked Bishop.

"No. Not really," Bishop replied. He almost added that the "divergence" she referred to made complete sense if the client had bogus receivables and inventory on its books. But he didn't. Bishop felt obligated to tread lightly because he didn't want to disrupt the timing of Wallace's plan to end BRIC's accounting fraud.

Chapter 11

Friday, January 17

Late on the evening of Friday, January 17, Bishop saved the electronic work paper file on which he had been working and opened the time spreadsheet file for the BRIC audit. It was that time of the week when Bishop entered the hours worked by each audit team member since 5 p.m. of the preceding week. After entering those hours, he prepared the weekly time and audit progress report and emailed it to Emma Nelson, who then forwarded the report to Jim Wilmeth and Cason Kellis.

The previous Friday morning, Emma Nelson had notified team members that, until further notice, the standard workday would be 8 a.m. to 8 p.m., including Saturday and Sunday, because the BRIC audit was woefully behind schedule. Eleven chargeable hours each day, weekends included, totaled 77 hours. After learning of Nelson's decision, Jim Wilmeth emailed the team members from his hospital client and told them that they could take three "personal" hours each week, which reduced their weekly workload to 74 hours.

As Bishop reviewed the individual time reports that had been emailed to him, he noticed that Emma Nelson had reported exactly 74 hours worked during the previous week. He knew that total was significantly understated. Bishop had worked 79 hours the previous week and Nelson was always in the conference room hard at work each morning when he arrived around 7:30 a.m. Two or three days per week, she ate lunch at the conference room table while she continued to work. Each evening, he observed her cramming work paper files into her bulging briefcase before she left for the night.

Bishop was certain that Nelson didn't report all of the hours she worked because she didn't want to bust her assigned time budgets and, in doing so, disappoint Cason Kellis. Eating time reduced Nelson's utilization rate that was a key factor in evaluating the overall performance of audit staff members—especially audit seniors. But her utilization rate was sky high anyway.

Ironically, while Emma Nelson was "eating" some of the time that she worked on the BRIC audit, Jim Wilmeth was inflating the number of hours that he charged to the engagement. How did Bishop know that? Because Wilmeth had told him.

One afternoon while the two of them were alone in the conference room, Wilmeth had matter-of-factly told Bishop that he would be "transferring" some of the hours that he had worked that week on the hospital audit to the BRIC engagement. He explained to Bishop that the hospital audit was a "fixed-fee" engagement, meaning that any excess hours on that job would be "written off" by the practice office. Plus, the negotiated fee was heavily discounted. Wilmeth told Bishop that the firm routinely extended such discounts to potential "high value" clients to "seal the deal." It was a "win-win situation," according to Wilmeth. Such "lowballing" ensured that the firm obtained stable and growing new clients that would be indebted to it, in a sense, and thus likely to be "loyal" audit clients in the foreseeable future. "It just makes good business sense," Wilmeth had remarked.

Because he didn't want any of his time "ditched," Wilmeth charged 15 to 20 hours that he worked on the hospital engagement each week to the BRIC job. Wilmeth told Bishop that audit partners and audit managers often "reallocated" the hours they worked on engagements to maximize the practice office's audit fee collections.

At first, Bishop thought that Wilmeth was teasing him. Surely, audit partners and audit managers wouldn't do something as ludicrous, if not criminal, as requiring certain clients to pay for time that had been spent working for other clients. But Wilmeth quickly convinced Bishop that was, in fact, the case. When Bishop asked him if the practice was "firm policy," Wilmeth replied, "Sure, but understand, you won't find it anywhere in the firm's policy manual. Here's the deal. As Kellis says, 'in the long run, it all evens out any way.' "

"Well it seems more than strange to me that you would bill a client for hours worked on another engagement," Bishop responded candidly.

"Michael," Wilmeth said with a touch of concern in his voice. "You understand that this is another one of those issues that has to be kept on the down low, right? Don't repeat what I have just told you to anyone."

"Sure, I understand," Bishop replied. "But, to me, it seems difficult to justify that sort of thing."

" 'Justify?' You've got to be kidding me," Wilmeth replied with a laugh. "The partners I have worked with are way beyond the point where they feel that they have to justify any of their questionable behavior. And that is absolutely true of Kellis. Besides, when you think about it, what's wrong with a huge company subsidizing the audit fees of smaller companies that are trying to get established? It even makes more sense for those big corporate clients to subsidize the audit fees of not-for-profits such as the new hospital client that I'm working on. Our firm isn't a charity, so why shouldn't it be compensated for the time that we work?"

After completing his mini-speech, Wilmeth laughed out loud again.

"What's so funny?" Bishop asked.

"Oh, it's just ironic. I bash Kellis all the time, but I'm starting to sound just like him. He's rubbing off on me."

"How so?"

"That charity 'line' is straight from Kellis. If you haven't already heard it, one of these days he will unload it on you. It goes something like this: 'First and foremost, don't ever forget that this firm is a business. If you want to work for a charity, the Salvation Army is always hiring.' If I've heard that once, I've heard it a dozen times."

The final time report that Bishop retrieved was from Becky Linton. Although she was dreadfully shy, Linton was a perfect staff accountant in many respects. She required little supervision, was technically competent, and never complained of the long hours that were often necessary in public accounting. Jackson Coleman, on the other hand, frequently commented on "returning to the salt mine" after lunch or an afternoon break and referred to the BRIC audit team as the "OJ brigade"—"OJ" was short for "orange jumpsuit." Earlier in the afternoon, Coleman had excused himself to take his three "personal" hours for the week. When Emma Nelson asked him how he would be spending those hours, Coleman had deadpanned, "I'm going to WalMart to buy some ricin to mix with my next Coke."

As Bishop entered the final few hours reported by Becky Linton, he recalled an incident a few days earlier involving her and Jim Wilmeth. The devout young lady spent her afternoon breaks reading her daily devotional from her Bible; the previous Sunday, she had used her three personal hours for the week to attend church services. Before each meal or snack, she closed her eyes, bowed her head, and said a brief prayer. During one such prayer while Linton, Coleman, Nelson, Wilmeth, and Bishop were having lunch together, Wilmeth had joked, "Becky, would you put in a good word with the Lord for me? I sure as hell need it."

Linton, who rarely spoke during a social gathering of the audit team, shocked everyone, including Wilmeth, by immediately and firmly replying, "Jim, I assure you that you're the first one on my prayer list every day."

Linton's comment served the purpose of chastening Wilmeth. For the remainder of the lunch, he was civil and respectful to his subordinates.

After completing the time and audit progress report, Bishop emailed it to Nelson, who was sitting a few feet away. Nelson was intensely studying the explanation of overhead application rates for BRIC's WIP inventory that she had found in the company's tattered, dog-eared, and coffee-stained Accounting Procedures and Policies Manual that was the size of a metro telephone directory. Earlier in the day, Bishop had overheard Jackson Coleman ask Nelson several pointed questions about the methods BRIC was using to apply overhead to its various WIP accounts.

"Emma, I think I will call it a night," Bishop said as he stood and began organizing his tabletop workspace. At the time, only Nelson and Bishop were in the conference room. Wilmeth, who had returned to BRIC's headquarters that morning after having spent the previous week at his hospital client, had left 45 minutes earlier.

"Okay, Michael. See you tomorrow morning," Nelson replied without looking up.

A short while later, as Bishop stepped toward the open door of the conference room, Nelson stopped him. "Could I speak to you for just a couple of minutes?"

"Sure, Emma, what's up?"

"Would you mind closing the door, please?"

After closing the door, Bishop sat on the edge of the conference room table while Nelson remained at the other end of the table, ten feet away.

"I just, uh, wanted to thank you," Nelson began. Bishop waited expectantly, having no idea of the source of Nelson's gratitude.

"Jim Wilmeth asked to speak to me this afternoon when you were spending some time working with Becky. He told me that you had suggested that he has been, to use his words, 'over the top' with me. He then apologized and promised that he would be more professional with me from now on." Nelson dabbed at her eyes before continuing. "I just wanted to thank you. That was very sweet of you to do that."

Bishop loosened his tie and then cleared his throat. Nelson was the only person on the audit team who had the ability to make him uncomfortable. "Well, you're welcome, Emma. I apologize for not having said something to him before."

Bishop had the sudden urge to ask Nelson to join him for dinner at Curcio's, the local pizza restaurant where they had eaten together several weeks earlier. But he thought the better of it. He didn't want to send the wrong signal to her. At the same time, Nelson was thinking of asking Bishop to join her for a late night meal. She didn't because she sensed that he might ask her instead.

Finally, after an extended pause, Nelson said "good night" to Bishop and then turned back to BRIC's enormous accounting manual.

As Michael Bishop made his way home that evening, thoughts of Emma Nelson and Jim Wilmeth were eclipsed by a growing uneasiness that he had been experiencing over the past week. Since meeting with Bud Wallace and his two attorneys more than three weeks earlier, Bishop had made every effort to avoid speaking with Wallace alone. When issues came up that required Wallace's help or input, Bishop first asked one of Wallace's subordinates. If that tactic failed, he would manufacture an excuse to ask a staff accountant on the BRIC audit team to accompany him to Wallace's office.

Despite steering clear of Wallace, Bishop had made a point over the past few weeks of observing the accounting manager when he interacted with the staff accountants on the BRIC audit team or with his own subordinates. The more he observed Wallace, the more Bishop became convinced that there was something unusual, if not strange, about him. Wallace's mode of interacting seemed contrived and less than authentic. Each time Wallace spoke to someone, it seemed as if he was playing a role rather than behaving spontaneously.

In recalling the two emotionally charged meetings with Wallace—at the Grotto and one week later when his two attorneys were present—Bishop gradually came to suspect that his behavior in each case had been less than genuine. As Bishop replayed those meetings in his mind, it seemed that Wallace's behavior had been overly dramatic, if not staged.

There was one other aspect of the second meeting that stuck in Bishop's mind. Wallace had briefly expressed concern that the state board of accountancy might learn of the BRIC accounting fraud and rescind his CPA certificate and those of the divisional controllers. Because Bishop had been in Wallace's office numerous times, he was well aware that there was no framed CPA certificate on display there. Most corporate accountants who have their own office proudly display their CPA certificate.

Several days after the December 23 meeting, Bishop accessed the online state registry of CPAs. Wallace's name was not listed on that website. He then accessed the CPA registries of three adjacent states. Once more, there was no CPA listed in those rosters under Wallace's name. Bishop realized that Wallace might have been certified in another state but chosen not to obtain a reciprocal CPA certificate in the state where BRIC Industries' headquarters was located. But he thought that was unlikely.

Bishop understood that Wallace's behavior and temperament might be a direct consequence of the enormous pressure that he was under given the personal crisis that he faced. Bishop even accepted the fact that his skepticism regarding Wallace was possibly a product of his own paranoia and growing uneasiness as the end of the BRIC audit approached. Despite all of that, by the time he reached his apartment, the audit senior had made a decision that he had been wrestling with the previous several days. He decided that he would call his former brother-in-law, Jack, who was a private detective. Although he hadn't spoken with Jack in more than two years, the two of them had always been on good terms. Bishop hoped that Jack would investigate Bud Wallace and determine whether there was any reason to question his credibility. At the very least, having Jack research Wallace's background would serve to eliminate one source of stress and concern as he prepared himself for the tumultuous conclusion of the BRIC audit.

Chapter 12

Wednesday, January 22

Early on a snowy Wednesday morning, Michael Bishop was flipping through Becky Linton's work papers for the sales and receivables accounts as he sat at the audit conference room table munching on a blueberry muffin and drinking a Mountain Dew. Emma Nelson was spending the morning and the early afternoon at the office with Lindsay Tankersley, the tax manager who was reviewing BRIC's deferred tax accounts. Nelson had told Bishop to "take charge" while she was away—Jim Wilmeth had indicated the day before that he would be at his hospital client "all of Wednesday if not Thursday."

Later that morning, Bishop would be meeting with Linton to discuss several issues that she had raised regarding the sales and receivables accounts. As Bishop studied the work papers for those accounts, he realized that it would be readily apparent to anyone who reviewed them that BRIC Industries was a master of "channel stuffing" and other gimmicks to inflate year-end sales.

During the final three days of the year, BRIC's shipping dock had operated around the clock preparing larger than normal sales shipments to dozens of the company's customers. Each of those customers had been granted a "seasonal" trade discount of five percent. That trade discount, which was applied to all December sales, had never been granted in the past and was in addition to the normal, volume-based trade discounts of 10 to 25 percent that the company extended to its customers.

Many of BRIC's late December sales shipments had left the company's shipping dock on common carriers with terms of FOB shipping point, but the shipments had not been delivered to the customers for more than two weeks. Instead, those shipments had been delivered to one of BRIC's regional distribution facilities scattered around the nation where the goods were eventually loaded on other trucks that would ultimately deliver them to the given customers. This "shipping to the yard" was not a new practice by BRIC, but the company had ramped up the volume of such shipments in the final two weeks of the year under audit.

There were several other red flags that suggested to Bishop that BRIC had intentionally inflated its December sales. The prior year audit work papers documented that similar tactics had been used in the past by BRIC but not to the same extent. Based upon some quick and crude extrapolations, Bishop estimated that at least one-half of BRIC's 13 percent year-over-year increase in December sales was due to the various sleights-of-hand applied by the company.

BRIC's vice-president of sales—who had been hired a few months after the company's new management team of Hakes, Zimmer, and Jennings was installed—had insisted to Linton that the significant increase in fourth-quarter sales, December sales, in particular, was simply a reflection of the rapidly improving national economy. Bishop's review of industry trade publications and news releases, however, revealed that BRIC's principal competitors had realized much more modest increases in fourth-quarter sales. The improving national economy was also the principal justification given by BRIC's sales staff to justify a sharp reduction in the year-end allowance for sales returns.

Self-serving representations by BRIC personnel had not been limited to the sales accounts. The company's curmudgeon of a credit manager had told Linton that falling unemployment and historically low interest rates were sufficient justification for him to lower the bad debt rates that the company applied to its aged accounts receivable. When Bishop asked the ill-mannered credit manager how BRIC's bad debt rates could be expected to fall given the sharp decrease in the company's receivables turnover ratio and the corresponding increase in its average collection period, the crotchety old man had at first stonewalled the audit senior just like he had done Linton previously. When Bishop continued to press the issue, the credit manager told him that he had "personally received assurance after assurance" from customers with past-due balances that they were going to "make good" on those balances "as soon as possible."

Because Bishop didn't want to speak with Bud Wallace unless absolutely necessary, many of the audit senior's questions regarding major accounting issues, such as aggressive revenue recognition practices and the collectability of accounts receivable, went unanswered. It had become increasingly apparent to Bishop that his and Nelson's avoidance of Wallace, the client employee most knowledgeable of BRIC's accounting issues, was impeding the progress of the audit and contributing to the time budgets being busted for many of the client's accounts.

There was no doubt in Bishop's mind that significant audit adjustments would have to be proposed for sales and accounts receivable. If the client, meaning Suzanne Jennings, refused to accept those adjustments, which she almost certainly would, the summary work paper memos for those accounts would have to conclude with adverse or qualified opinions, which would cause Cason Kellis to blow a gasket.

Bishop wanted to do everything possible to avoid being forced to "nudge"— Bud Wallace's term—Kellis into contesting BRIC's fourth-quarter earnings. Bishop wanted the BRIC disaster to come and go without him becoming a focal point of attention. That would allow him to ride out the storm and remain employed by his firm. If he had to become an active participant in Wallace's grand scheme to end BRIC's accounting fraud, he would almost certainly lose his job.

An underperforming audit senior who clashed with an audit partner would be shown the door, and quickly.

The timing of the wrap-up audit procedures for the BRIC audit and Wallace's timeline for ending Jennings' accounting fraud gave Bishop some hope that he could avoid becoming a central figure in Wallace's plot. Many of those wrap-up procedures, including preparing the final "polished" versions of the summary work paper memos for individual accounts, were typically completed after the date that the audit partner gave the client the "okay" to issue its earnings press release. BRIC intended to issue its earnings press release on Monday, February 24, and file its 10-K with the SEC on Friday, February 28, while Wallace intended to detonate his inventory "grenade" sometime prior to Friday, February 21.

Bishop realized that Cason Kellis and Jim Wilmeth were scheduled to review the BRIC audit work papers during the week of February 17-21. He planned to do everything possible to delay their review of investments and long-term debt, the two accounts that were his direct responsibility, until Wallace had revealed the large inventory overstatement. Although, neither of his accounts was a major focus of the BRIC accounting fraud, Bishop had uncovered several questionable accounting decisions that had been made for those accounts that would require him to propose audit adjustments.

Once Wallace revealed the large misstatement of inventory, that issue would almost certainly take center stage, meaning that the attention of Kellis and Wilmeth would be diverted from the other client accounts. If Kellis decided that a large adjustment to inventory was necessary due to the problem revealed by Wallace, then he would likely be more receptive to material adjustments for other BRIC accounts. At that point, Kellis might actually adopt a defensive point of view and insist that those accounts be reported at conservative amounts.

On the other hand, Kellis might cave in to Jennings regardless of Wallace's shocking inventory revelation. In that case, Bishop wasn't sure what he would do. At that point, he might be forced to attempt to convince Kellis that there were pervasive problems in BRIC's accounting records.

In fact, Bishop recognized that it was next to impossible to predict what would happen over the next few weeks. What was undeniable were the major problems being uncovered by the BRIC auditors that were ticking time bombs in the audit work papers thanks to the lack of communication between Emma Nelson and her two superiors. Although Jim Wilmeth was treating Nelson more civilly, the two seldom discussed important issues that were arising on the BRIC audit, in large part because Wilmeth was preoccupied with his new hospital client. During Cason Kellis's brief Friday afternoon visits to the audit conference room, the audit partner subverted any attempt by Nelson to discuss the BRIC audit and instead insisted on engaging in small talk with the attractive audit senior.

Bishop's overview of the sales and receivables work papers was interrupted when Kaimee Mongold stepped into the audit conference room and handed him her cell phone and a post-it note.

"Michael, that phone call you have been expecting just came in. Here's the number you are supposed to call."

"Oh, thanks a lot Kaimee. I will return your phone in a few minutes."

Two days earlier, on Monday morning, Bishop had borrowed Kaimee's cell phone to call his former brother-in-law. He had told Kaimee, who was nearby helping Becky Linton clear accounts receivable confirmations, that his cell phone had been going "on the blink" and that he didn't have time to get it repaired. In truth, Bishop was simply being cautious. He didn't want to place or receive any sensitive calls on his own cell phone.

"Hello Jack. How are you?"

"I'm good, Michael. I have some information for you. Are you somewhere where you can talk?"

"Yes, no problem, go ahead." Bishop had placed the call from a vacant alcove of the employee break room.

"William Earl Wallace, or, Bud Wallace, as you know him, was born in Tampa, Florida. His father and mother still live there. His father is a vascular surgeon in Ocala, Florida, who has been practicing there for thirty-six years."

A knot formed in Michael Bishop's stomach as he learned that Bud Wallace's sorrowful story about his father was false.

"You there, Michael?"

"Yes. Go ahead."

"Seven years ago, Wallace was indicted by the Florida state attorney general for selling unregistered securities in the state of Florida. He pleaded guilty to two counts of violating state securities laws, paid a fine of $25,000 and received a two-year suspended prison sentence. Six months after the case was settled, Wallace legally changed his name to William Earl Wallace. His birth name was Joseph Thomas Wallace, Jr. He is known as 'Joe' by friends and family members."

By this time, Bishop felt physically sick. He knew that his life had taken a sudden change for the worse. The accounting gimmicks being perpetrated by BRIC Industries were now the least of his worries.

"Wallace was previously a CPA. He passed the CPA exam in Florida twelve years ago, but he voluntarily surrendered his certificate and license to practice after pleading guilty to the fraud charges. I couldn't find any indication that the state board took any further action against him."

"Well, Jack, this guy has really conned me." Bishop's voice was tinged with embarrassment and regret.

"Michael, listen to me. I want you to do something. I'm going to give you the number of an FBI agent who is stationed in an FBI field office less than five miles from where you live. I've known this guy for fifteen years since we were in college together. He's solid as a rock. His name is Jake Doolin."

After giving Bishop the FBI agent's phone number, Jack continued. "No one wants to become involved in an FBI investigation, but this is an extremely serious situation. At this point in time, you can disengage yourself from this mess if you will cooperate with the FBI. There is no way that you will face any repercussions if you act now. Okay?"

"Okay, Jack. I understand and I will place that call as soon as I hang up."

"One more thing."

"Sure, Jack. Go ahead."

"Whatever you do, you have to be stone-cold honest with the FBI and any other law enforcement officials. Don't embellish facts, don't stretch the truth, don't take the risk of speculating about anything. If you are asked a question that you don't know the answer to, admit it. Any mistakes in judgment that you have made, you have to spell them out in detail. Don't give the feds any reason to doubt your honesty."

"I hear you Jack. I understand."

"Michael, you're going to be fine. The FBI will make arrangements to meet with you. Don't place any calls to the FBI on your cell phone."

"Okay."

"Hey, brother, I'm here for you," Jack reassured Bishop. "And I know how tough you are. You are going to make it through this just fine."

"Jack, I can't thank you enough. When I have a chance, I will call you."

Chapter 13

Saturday, January 25

"Emma, I need to take a few hours this afternoon to run several errands that have piled up over the last couple of weeks. Is that okay?" Michael Bishop asked Emma Nelson shortly after the two of them arrived at the audit conference room on Saturday morning.

"Michael. You're the only one of us who hasn't taken any personal hours since Jim set up that policy. Take as many hours as you need. And you didn't need to ask me."

"Well, hey, better to be safe than sorry," Bishop responded with a smile.

Saturday and Sunday were casual days, which explained why both Bishop and Nelson were decked out in jeans and t-shirts as they sat across from each other at the conference room table—unlike Bishop's standard gray athletic tee, Nelson's "t-shirt" was a gaudy short-sleeved blouse decorated with spangles and sequins that she had likely purchased at an *haute couture* shop.

"I have been meaning to ask you, Michael. Has Becky had any time to begin working on reconciling vendor statements to the accounts payable sub-ledger?"

"In fact, just yesterday I sat down with her and we came up with a plan for selecting the twenty vendors for that test," Bishop replied. "Last year, the auditors selected a random sample of twenty open payables accounts for that test. This year, Becky and I decided that she would apply the reconciliation procedure to the ten largest payables balances at year-end and then choose another ten balances haphazardly—you know, randomly but not 'randomly,' in an auditing sense."

"Is she going to start that test soon?"

"Well, she is spending most of her time right now trying to clear all the exceptions on the receivables confirmations that have been flooding in the past week. But I told her that she should probably take a couple of hours this weekend to begin organizing the vendor statement reconciliation test. I suggested that she sit down this coming Monday with Yong-Mi, the head payables clerk, and become familiar with how the payables files are organized. Yong-Mi is very helpful and will spend the time necessary to get Becky up to speed on the payables account. I told Becky that she could then ask one of the internal auditors working with us to begin pulling the selected files so that she will have a head start on the payables reconciliations when she breaks free from receivables."

"That sounds good," Emma responded. "What about the search for unrecorded liabilities? Have you and Becky discussed that test?"

"I wouldn't say we have 'discussed' it. I reminded Becky that as soon as she completes the vendor reconciliations that she has to start working on the reasonableness tests for the major accrued liabilities and get them out of the way so that she can begin the search for unrecorded liabilities during the first week of February. Because we are going to use a six-week window for the search, it doesn't make much sense for her to start that test before the end of January."

Nelson and Bishop were now working together smoothly, but Nelson continued to struggle with the insecurity and immaturity of the staff accountants, particularly the four rookies. Over the previous several weeks, Bishop had overheard Nelson on multiple occasions scold individual rookies by telling them that they needed to demonstrate more "initiative" and to assume more "ownership" for the tasks they had been assigned.

Because Nelson didn't enjoy supervising the staff accountants, she and Bishop had recently agreed on a new division of responsibilities for that task. Bishop assumed the principal responsibility for supervising Linton and the four rookie staff accountants assigned to the BRIC engagement, while Nelson would deal with the questions and issues raised by Coleman Jackson who was spending practically all of his time working on the inventory accounts. In exchange for Bishop assuming the bulk of the supervisory responsibilities for the staff accountants, Nelson agreed to complete most of the tasks that she had earlier jointly assigned to herself and Bishop, such as the preparation of the attorneys' letters. This arrangement suited Bishop just fine since he wanted to avoid the problematic inventory accounts that were central to Bud Wallace's plan to end BRIC's accounting fraud.

The increased supervisory burden imposed on Bishop meant that he had to work on his assigned accounts in 15 to 20 minute spurts throughout the day. As the audit progressed, he found himself staying later and later each night after the staff accountants had left so that he could focus uninterrupted on those accounts for a span of an hour or longer. Over the previous few days, he and Nelson had not left the audit conference room before 10 p.m. Each night, they had a pizza or Chinese take-out delivered to the front door of BRIC's headquarters and spent dinner together while they worked on their respective tasks.

On this particular Saturday morning, the BRIC audit was not Bishop's major concern since that afternoon he would be meeting with one or more agents of the Federal Bureau of Investigation. Those five words seemed to be on a revolving marquee that was circulating around and around inside his head. Each time they passed through his memory banks, a surge of fear-fed adrenaline was released into his veins. He hoped that the meeting would be quick and uneventful; he knew it wouldn't be.

———————

Shortly after noon, Bishop arrived at the huge suburban mall a few miles from BRIC's headquarters and made his way to the food court where he ordered a plate of sliders and onion rings. Twenty-five minutes later, he was window shopping along the third-floor promenade of the monstrous mall waiting for the all-clear sign.

As Bishop circled the promenade for the second time, he glanced at a man near the entrance of a major department store—the man, who fit the mold of a soccer dad, was wearing a solid green t-shirt. The first time that Bishop passed the man, he had been standing next to the railing of the promenade, gazing at the large skating rink three floors below in the mall's basement. This time, the man was facing the other direction reading a newspaper. That was the all-clear sign. Once the FBI had determined that Bishop wasn't being followed, he had been instructed to proceed to a door marked "Private" halfway down a third-floor corridor that led to public restrooms.

The day before, on Friday morning, Bishop had stopped by a local 7-11 on his way to BRIC's headquarters, which he did every morning. As he reached inside the cooler to retrieve a Gatorade, a young man passed by him and deftly placed a folded, unmarked envelope in his hand, which Bishop casually slipped into a pocket of his trousers. A few minutes later, while he sat in his car in the BRIC Industries parking garage, Bishop read the note that contained the instructions he was to follow to meet with the FBI. On the way to the audit conference room, Bishop ripped the note to shreds and flushed it down a toilet.

———————

After pushing open the door marked "Private," Bishop turned and walked down a narrow hallway to his right. At the end of the hallway sat two men in their early thirties. Each of them was wearing starched jeans and a starched dress shirt.

"Hello, Michael. I'm Jake. I'm the fellow who is the friend of your former brother-in-law, Jack Conatser." Jake had a firm handshake and a piercing gaze. Bishop immediately sensed that the agent was sizing him up.

"This is Lee," Jake said as he motioned to the burr-headed, muscular young man to his left.

"Hello Michael. Glad to meet you."

The three of them sat down in molded plastic chairs that surrounded a wobbly dinette table that appeared to be a reject from Goodwill Industries. A few moments later, the agent in the green-colored t-shirt walked into the cozy meeting room and introduced himself as "Wayne."

"Michael, first of all, I want to assure you that you absolutely did the right thing by contacting us," Jake began.

"Well, I feel bad that I was, uh, hoodwinked by this guy Wallace. He was pretty convincing."

"These con men are like that. They can fool the best of us. Even auditors," Jake added with an understanding smile.

"I appreciate that, sir. I just want you to know that I'm here to fully cooperate." Bishop was tense but composed.

"Hey, we are all on a first-name basis here. And understand that we are all on the same team. So, just relax. I know it's not every day that you sit down with some G-men." Jake was doing his best to make Bishop feel comfortable. "You might be surprised, but the three of us are all accountants by training. In fact, Wayne, here, worked for three years as an auditor for a Big Four firm before joining the Bureau."

"Speaking of which, how is that audit going, Michael?" Wayne asked.

Bishop hesitated as the phrase "client confidentiality" raced through his mind. Then he recalled the advice that Jack had given him. "Not very well at all, to be honest."

"Okay. Well, we will explore that with you later," Wayne replied.

"Michael, let's get to the heart of the matter." The tone of Jake's voice and his body language suggested that the friendly chit-chat was finished. "First of all, everything that will be said here must be totally confidential. You cannot discuss what goes on here. You cannot tell anyone, and I mean anyone, that you even met us. Do you understand?"

"Yes, sir. I mean, yes … Jake." Bishop's head felt as if it was stuffed with cotton candy. He tried to clear his mind because he knew that he had to give the FBI agents his undivided attention.

"This is an extremely serious matter," Jake continued. "A situation that involves an insider trading scheme and huge sums of money. Bud Wallace is a key participant in that scheme."

Bishop wearily shook his head and exhaled. That reaction prompted Jake to ask Bishop a question.

"Did you have some reason to suspect that this might involve insider trading?"

Bishop wished that he had not shown any reaction to Jake's statement about insider trading. But it was too late at this point.

"Yes, I raised that issue several weeks ago during a meeting with Wallace and two fellows who were supposed to be his attorneys." Bishop's statements caused a flurry of typing by Lee, the agent manning a laptop computer who was apparently the appointed stenographer for the meeting. Bishop was unsure why Lee was taking notes because Jake had placed a small audio recording device in plain sight on the table.

"Do you happen to recall those attorneys' names and can you give us physical descriptions of them?"

Bishop was asked to recall every detail, even some of the most remote and seemingly insignificant details of his meeting with Bud Wallace in the Grotto and the December 23 meeting with Wallace and his alleged attorneys. The agents asked him to describe not only the physical appearance of "Charles" and "Zed" but also the bartender who had fed Wallace the gin and tonics at the Grotto. They asked him to describe each time he had spoken to Wallace at BRIC headquarters, both prior to and after the Grotto meeting. They wanted to know why Emma Nelson seemed to dislike Wallace, a question that Bishop couldn't answer. They asked Bishop to provide any information or insight that he could regarding Wallace's relationship with Suzanne Jennings, Jameson Hardy, the divisional controllers, and anyone else with whom he had seen Wallace interact at BRIC headquarters including accounting clerks, secretaries, maintenance personnel, and even outside couriers. Finally, they quizzed Bishop at length regarding Wallace's plan to end the accounting fraud.

Next, the agents began grilling Bishop about his coworkers on the BRIC audit team. For at least 20 minutes, they questioned him regarding Cason Kellis and Jim Wilmeth. They wanted to know what he thought of them on both a professional and personal level. The agents had so much interest in Kellis and Wilmeth that Bishop began wondering whether they suspected that the audit partner and audit manager might be involved in the insider trading scheme.

The agents then turned their attention to Emma Nelson. "Was she psychologically stable?" "How did she interact with Kellis and Wilmeth?" "On a professional level, do you believe she is competent?" "On a personal level, do you believe she is trustworthy?" "Have you ever discovered her lying to you?" "Is it apparent when she is being dishonest?" On and on the questions went and each answer by Bishop prompted a burst of typing by Lee.

The questions regarding Jackson Coleman, Becky Linton, the four rookie accountants, Paula Henderson, and John Kelly were fewer in number and less intense, although the romantic relationship between Nelson and Kelly piqued the agents' interest and led to a line of questions that made Bishop uncomfortable.

"What about you and Nelson?" Wayne asked. "Is there any romantic or possible romantic involvement there?"

"Uh, no." Bishop reconsidered his answer and then responded more firmly, "No."

Neither Jake nor Wayne seemed satisfied with Bishop's answer. "Are you sure?" Jake asked. "You said she is, to use your words, 'very attractive.' That sounds like someone who would interest most available males."

The tone of Jake's question raised another unspoken question, at least in Bishop's mind.

"Well, if you're asking about my sexual orientation, I, uh, I'm heterosexual."

"Okay," Jake nodded before pursuing the topic even more aggressively. "So, why aren't you interested in Nelson? You are handsome and age appropriate. It seems to me that you would be, or should be, interested in her."

Bishop got the impression that the agents weren't so much interested in his feelings, or lack thereof, for Emma Nelson, but rather were pursuing the topic because they believed he was being less than forthcoming.

"Well. Okay. I mean, sure, she's, uh, adorable physically. But …"

"But she's not your type?" Jake asked as he cocked his head at an angle and leaned forward slightly.

"Okay. I am just trying to be honest here. No, Emma isn't my type. We are from very different backgrounds. But I guess … that I could foresee some set of circumstances, you know, where something might develop between the two of us. Like, sometime in the future."

"And that would be okay with you?" Wayne chipped in.

"Uh, sure. I guess so. I mean, I'm not going out of my way to get involved with anyone at this point in my life. But, yes, it's possible that Emma and I could, you know …" Bishop hesitated as he extended his hands with his palms turned upward.

Suddenly, the awkward and embarrassing line of questions ended. Bishop wondered to himself if his body language had communicated something to the agents, something that had finally satisfied them.

———————

The final person that the FBI agents wanted to discuss was Bishop himself. They asked about his upbringing, his family life, his teenage years. Bishop became increasingly stressed as they came closer and closer to the time frame when he had lost his son. For the first time, he wouldn't have the option of not discussing his son's death.

"I'm sorry that we have to ask you this," Jake said before his first question regarding Ollie. Somehow, Bishop got through the questions without breaking down. It wasn't easy. On multiple occasions, he had to force himself to focus on the specific question being asked and to drive the thoughts of his handsome and happy little son from his mind.

Several questions later, after Jake had moved on and began questioning Bishop about his final years in college, the FBI agent suddenly returned to Ollie.

"You miss your son enormously, don't you Michael?" Before giving Bishop sufficient time to respond, Jake fired off a series of rapid fire questions, none of which Bishop had adequate time to answer before he was slammed by the next question.

"How does the loss of your son affect your outlook on your job and career in public accounting?" "Do you feel as if you are always in control of your emotions?" "Do you become depressed for extended periods of time?" "Have you ever felt suicidal?"

The relentless string of harsh questions pounded like a sledgehammer at Bishop's psyche, but he answered each of them truthfully. Later, he would realize that the questions were intended by the agents to see how he would react in the most stressful of situations. But, at the time, he thought the questions were unnecessary and inappropriate, if not cruel.

After Jake stopped peppering Bishop with questions related to Ollie, Bishop lowered his head and then cleared his throat before volunteering a few candid thoughts on the loss of his son.

"I miss my son desperately. I guess that you could say that I have never dealt with that loss properly." Bishop lifted his head and gazed steadily into Jake's eyes. "Like I said, sometimes I am down or blue for a while. But I recover soon enough. And then, I go on with my life."

In those few moments, Bishop had voluntarily spoken about his son's death for the first time to someone other than his former wife, mother, and sister. Although he felt numb, he felt more focused than ever.

After a long and tortuous pause, Jake picked up with the line of questions regarding Bishop's college years. During the meeting and from that point on, Jake and the other agents never asked another question about Ollie, never mentioned him or alluded to him or his death or how his death had impacted or continued to impact Bishop.

The inquisition ended with Wayne, the former auditor among the three agents, asking Bishop a series of detailed questions about the BRIC Industries audit. Among other questions, he asked what major problems had been discovered to that point in the audit, whether Kellis or Wilmeth seemed concerned by those problems, and to what degree Wallace and other key company personnel were cooperating with the auditors. Finally, Wayne asked Bishop to lay out the planned timeline for completing the audit.

After the questions ended, the three agents excused themselves and left Bishop sitting alone at the dinette table. Bishop checked his wristwatch; it was a quarter past three. His three-hour personal break would officially end in 45 minutes. Although he knew that Emma Nelson wouldn't question him if he returned later than 4 p.m., he hoped that he would be back in the audit conference room by then. The meeting with the FBI agents had proven to be much more stressful than he had anticipated and there was no indication that the agents were done with him.

Ten minutes passed before the agents returned and sat back down at the dinette table. In his hand, Jake held a pocket-sized notebook in which he had scribbled several notes.

"Michael, over the past seventy-two hours, we have done an extensive and extremely thorough background investigation of you. That investigation has led the three of us in this room, our superiors in our field office, and FBI officials in Washington, D.C., to decide that you are trustworthy and a man of integrity." Jake paused as he peered into Bishop's eyes.

Bishop wasn't sure whether he was supposed to respond; he wasn't sure how to respond. So, he said nothing.

"You are about to join a very small club, an exclusive fraternity. We are going to share top secret information with you that only a few individuals possess."

Jake paused again to allow Bishop to process what he had just said.

"You have stumbled upon an international network that engages in insider trading. This organization is extremely secretive. We have been investigating it for several years, and we still know very little about it. This organization is so secretive that its members don't even have a name for it. At the FBI, we simply refer to it as the Agency. The members of the Agency rarely communicate by email, by cell phone, or by any other means by which their communications could be intercepted. We know that in the United States they often communicate by traveling from location to location to exchange verbal messages in person. They may have someone fly across the country or even drive several hundred miles to deliver a brief message."

The FBI believed that the Agency made several billion dollars each year in the U.S. alone from insider trading transactions, but that number was little more than a guess and the actual figure could be much higher. The Agency obtained inside information regarding public companies and then used that information to earn stock market gains. Because the Agency's operatives were very familiar with the complex events processing (CEP) software used by the SEC to detect insider trading activity, they seldom activated the triggers embedded in that software. The key tactic they used to avoid activating those triggers was limiting the amount of trading volume in the stock of any given "target company." The Agency was generally satisfied with earning a moderate gain on any one stock because of the large number of companies that it targeted. "Amateur" inside traders, on the other hand, typically attempted to make a "big killing" on the stock of a given company, a strategy that greatly increased the likelihood they would be detected and prosecuted by federal authorities.

Public companies that were likely engaging in earnings management or blatantly fraudulent accounting schemes were common targets of the Agency. Such schemes inflated the prices of the given companies' stocks but made it almost inevitable that those stock prices would drop sharply when the scams were either discontinued or publicly exposed. After identifying a target company, the Agency would obtain confidential information confirming that the company was misrepresenting its financial statements. The Agency relied primarily on paid informants—often members of the given company's accounting staff—to funnel such information to them.

After confirming that a target company was distorting its reported operating results, the Agency would begin short selling the company's common stock. When the accounting fraud or earnings management scheme was exposed or otherwise ended and the company's stock price fell, the Agency would close the outstanding short positions by purchasing the stock, thereby locking in a gain. The FBI suspected that the Agency was somehow involved in terminating the accounting scams of most of its target companies.

Joint investigations by the FBI and SEC suggested that the Agency went to great lengths to identify companies that were predisposed toward manipulating their earnings—even before those companies began distorting their reported earnings. BRIC Industries was a classic example of such a company. It was a formerly high-flying company whose revenue growth had slowed dramatically and whose gross margins on its major products had narrowed significantly due to increased competition. In such cases, a disappointed board of directors often replaced its company's management team with a squad of turnaround specialists who had a track record of reviving companies with "tired" or "broken" business models. The hiring of such a management team, according to the FBI agents, was one of the most common precursors to creative or fraudulent accounting schemes.

When BRIC's board hired the troika of Hakes, Zimmer, and Jennings to resuscitate the company, the Agency had identified BRIC as a target company. Months earlier, when rumors began circulating that BRIC's board intended to overhaul its senior management team, the FBI had decided that the Agency would eventually choose BRIC as a target company.

The FBI was certain that Bud Wallace was the BRIC Industries insider who the Agency had tabbed as its paid informant. He was a malcontent with a well-concealed criminal record who believed that he was underpaid and underappreciated by his employer. A bitter divorce had left Wallace even more disillusioned and susceptible to the Agency. According to the agents, Wallace had likely been promised a pay-off in the low six digits if the stock swindle involving BRIC Industries was successful.

Over the prior 12 months, the Agency had apparently sold a disproportionately large—by its standards—volume of BRIC common stock under the assumption that there would eventually be a large correction (decline) in the stock's price. The FBI and the SEC had spent enormous time and effort attempting to determine which of the BRIC short sellers were involved with the Agency.

In recent months, the FBI had discovered evidence that suggested the Agency had such a large "overhang" of short positions in BRIC's stock that the organization was desperate to unwind or close those positions. An opportunity had arisen to close out those positions when BRIC's weak reported operating results for the third quarter had caused the company's stock price to drop by 15 percent. But the Agency had held its ground, effectively betting that the stock price would fall even further. Instead, the stock price had rallied due to the series of upbeat press releases issued by BRIC's management.

Making matters much worse for the Agency were the recent rumors that a private equity firm was planning to purchase BRIC's outstanding stock and take the company private. If that happened, the Agency would not only forfeit the huge gains that it had anticipated, it would incur losses in the tens of millions of dollars when it was forced to close its open positions in advance of the buy-out by the private equity firm.

According to Jake, the Agency had probably instructed Wallace to recruit Bishop to ensure that the accounting fraud was ended before the buyout took place. The Agency would not take the risk of anonymously exposing the fraud because that would encourage the SEC and law enforcement authorities to suspect an insider trading scam. Likewise, the Agency couldn't have Wallace contact the SEC and blow the whistle on the fraud because that would almost certainly trigger a criminal investigation of him that might result in the Agency's cover being blown.

———————

Jake explained to Bishop that the FBI and SEC officials had decided that he was perfectly positioned to provide extremely useful information and insights regarding the Agency. Because the Agency's operations undercut the credibility of the nation's capital markets, the organization posed a threat to the nation's free market economic system. The two federal agencies and the handful of top legislative officials who knew of the Agency's existence were committed to destroying it.

"Do you understand now why it is so imperative that everything that has been said to you in this room must be strictly confidential?" Jake asked as he stared intently at Bishop.

"Yes. Yes, I do," Bishop responded firmly.

"I want to lay out for you what is going to take place over the next several days." Jake leaned back in his chair momentarily to review his scribbled notes. "We want you to maintain your normal schedule and routine. Within the next three days, you will be given another message when you stop at your neighborhood convenience store in the morning. That message will inform you of the time and location of another meeting that we will have with you within the next week. The meeting will have to be held during work hours, so you will have to use your personal hours again."

"Okay, I can do that," Bishop responded.

"At that meeting, we will be prepared to tell you how we want you to help us. In the meantime, here's a secure cell phone that you can use to contact us if an emergency arises." Jake handed the cell phone to Bishop along with a list of phone numbers for himself and the two other agents. "We will be doing a sweep of your apartment to determine whether you are under surveillance. You will be under twenty-four hour surveillance by us. You should also know that we will initiate surveillance of your audit conference room."

Bishop wondered how the FBI would gain access to the audit conference room, but he wasn't about to ask.

"Again, Michael, it is absolutely imperative that you don't vary from your normal routine," Jake continued. "You must maintain that subdued, calm, and cool disposition that you have become known for by your colleagues and other acquaintances. It is extremely important that no one senses an overt change in your mood or temperament. Is that understood?"

"Yes, I understand. I understand completely."

"Michael, if you hurry, you can make it back to your conference room by 4 p.m. Before you leave, do you have any questions, understanding that it is unlikely that we can answer them at this point?"

"No, I don't. I'm good."

Chapter 14

Friday, January 31

While the other members of the audit team were at lunch, Michael Bishop sat in the audit conference room leafing through a stack of brokerage statements that he was using to vouch the year-end market values assigned to BRIC's long-term investments. He paused for a few moments to finish the last few bites of a tuna salad sandwich that he had fished out of a vending machine in the break room. Bishop was working through lunch to partially compensate for the time that he would be away from BRIC headquarters that afternoon.

Late Thursday morning, Bishop had told Emma Nelson that he planned to take three personal hours on Friday afternoon. Before Nelson could respond, Jim Wilmeth told Bishop that he was canceling the "personal time policy" because the BRIC audit was so far behind schedule.

"Jim, I have already made arrangements to meet someone," Bishop responded.

For the first time in Bishop's presence, Wilmeth asserted his managerial authority. "Michael, I can't ask the other team members to skip their personal breaks if you don't as well. You're an audit senior now. You have to set an example for the staff below you."

"Sorry, Jim," Bishop replied, "but, like I said, I've already made arrangements to meet someone." Bishop left out the fact that the "someone" he would be meeting included federal law enforcement officials who, at that very moment, were recording everything that was being said in the conference room.

"So, you are telling me that you're going to take a break even though I have specifically told you not to?" Wilmeth snapped. All morning, it had been apparent that Wilmeth was upset about something. Bishop was now the victim of the audit manager's displaced anger.

"Jim, in the month of January, my utilization rate is going to approach, if not exceed, two hundred percent. But, if you insist, I will make up the three hours that I will be gone tomorrow afternoon."

In the past, Bishop had served as a referee between Nelson and Wilmeth, but now Emma Nelson was forced to assume the role of peacemaker.

"Guys, we are all worn out, frustrated, and upset, so let's just calm down and take a deep breath." Nelson glanced at Bishop before turning to face Wilmeth. "Jim, I agree with Michael. Last week was the first time that he had taken any personal hours. I don't believe there is anything wrong with Michael being gone for a few hours tomorrow afternoon, especially since he has already made a commitment to meet someone."

"Good golly, let's see here. Two against one. Guess I'm outvoted. Didn't know we had formed our own little democracy here."

"Jim, there is no reason to make a big deal out of this." Bishop was angry but his calm tone and demeanor masked that anger. "I apologize if my leaving is going to be inconvenient or send the wrong signal to the other team members. But, again, I will make up the time. And I will talk to each of the staff accountants and tell them that I will be making up the three hours. Plus, if you want, I will personally inform them that, beginning tomorrow, there will be no more of the excessive three-hour personal breaks that are responsible for us being hopelessly behind schedule on this audit."

Bishop's cynical humor caused Wilmeth to briefly smile and persuaded the audit manager to end the confrontation without firing another volley.

Nelson and Bishop would later learn from the office rumor mill that Jim Wilmeth had met with Todd Wilson the day before, on Wednesday evening. At that meeting, Wilson had told Wilmeth that he would have until June 30 to find another job. Wilmeth had not taken the news well despite the fact that he had known for some time that he eventually would be asked to leave the firm.

Less than one hour after the confrontation between Bishop and Wilmeth on Thursday morning, two of the rookie staff accountants on the BRIC audit team walked into the audit conference room and announced that the following day, the final day of January, would be their last day with the firm. Both of them had accepted jobs with a large metropolitan bank and would be attending a six-week long commercial lending course that began the following Monday in their new employer's downtown training facility.

"You got to be kidding me. You can't quit in the middle of an audit," Wilmeth had responded angrily.

"Yes we can and yes we are," one of the rookies replied without wavering. "When we accepted this job, no one told us that we would be working nearly eighty hours per week. You may not understand, but that doesn't appeal to us." Before Wilmeth could respond, the determined young lady added, "We explained the situation to the HR people at our new employer and they are fine with our decision to resign before the audit is completed."

After the two staff accountants left, a dour Wilmeth told Nelson to call the office and request that two "floaters" be sent to BRIC headquarters the following Monday.

After Wilmeth left the audit conference room at 8 p.m. on Thursday evening, Nelson invited Bishop to have dinner with her at Curcio's. During their meal, Nelson revealed that she had never felt more stressed.

"Michael, this audit has turned into a disaster and I have no idea how it is going to end. We are way behind schedule on all of the major tests and we only have three and a half weeks left before Suzanne Jennings issues the press release that announces the company's earnings for the fourth quarter and the entire year."

"Emma, I don't know what to tell you," Bishop responded. "You know, we got off to a late start, Kellis and Wilmeth haven't been committed to the engagement, and the client has been much less than helpful. All in all, it has been a rough ride."

Nelson nodded in agreement before leaning forward and whispering, "To be honest, I am beginning to doubt that it's even possible for us to issue an unqualified opinion on BRIC's financial statements. There are so many problems with inventory alone. We have spent hundreds of hours auditing inventory, and I have no clue whether the number they intend to report is even in the ballpark. In fact, sometimes I have this strange feeling that the client is intentionally overstating inventory."

As the conversation continued, Nelson asked Bishop whether he thought there might be a coordinated effort by the client to overstate inventory. Bishop, who did not want to be sucked into a discussion of BRIC's fraudulent inventory accounts, responded by telling Nelson that he had not "reviewed" the results of the inventory audit tests, a statement intended to gently remind her that as the supervising audit senior she was responsible for reviewing those work papers.

Because she was concerned that BRIC's year-end in-transit inventory was much larger than normal, Nelson asked Bishop if there were any audit tests he was aware of that they could use to confirm the in-transit inventory after the fact. Bishop initially balked at answering her question, but then, after his conscience got the better of him, suggested that an inventory rollback might be helpful. Nelson had never performed an inventory rollback. When Bishop told her that rollbacks were tedious and time-consuming, she lost interest in performing the test.

"Well, that squelches that idea. We need more audit evidence for inventory, but there's no way to justify using a lot of time to collect it since we have used almost all of the budgeted hours for the inventory accounts and it's only the end of January."

Because he felt sorry for Nelson, Bishop decided to give her some advice that might be helpful. "Maybe you should go to Kellis and tell him how you feel. Just tell him point blank that you are very concerned about the reliability of the client's key account balances, especially inventory. If you do that, then you will have covered your bases."

"Michael, because Jim Wilmeth has been absent so much and because we don't have much of a relationship, I have made a point of trying to keep Kellis informed of every major problem that we have experienced. You know, he calls me every few days just to 'chat.'" Nelson rolled her eyes and softly shook her head. It was her first admission that Cason Kellis had a personal interest in her. Surprisingly, Nelson then breached the subject directly. "I don't know why so many men treat me like some sex object. I just want to do my job and be a professional like everyone else."

Bishop hoped he wasn't sexist, but a thought that might be considered sexist did roll through his mind, namely, that Nelson was partially to blame for the unwanted attention that she received from the men with whom she worked. Sitting there across from him at the table, she was dazzling, as usual. She was decked out in a beautiful turquoise blouse made of some translucent fabric, an underlying silk chemise, and a charcoal skirt that could only be described as less than modest given its snugness and shortness.

"Anyway, getting back to my original point," Nelson continued, "I have tried to tell him about the difficulty we have had trying to tie the receivables controlling account to the total of the subsidiary ledger, I have tried to tell him about the large number of exceptions in the inventory price tests and the receivables confirmations. More than once, I tried to tell him that the exception rates for the internal control tests were too high and that we should expand some of the other audit tests as a result."

An exasperated Nelson propped her right elbow on the table and then rested her chin on her open palm. "But each time I try to talk to him about the audit, he changes the subject. Just a few days ago, he cut me off when I began referring to the audit. He then told me that if he is appointed the head of that proposed biotech group, I will be the first senior he chooses to join his team. He said something totally disgusting like, 'That would give us the opportunity to spend a lot of time together in the future.'"

"Ugh. That is disgusting, Emma. I'm sorry." Bishop didn't feel that he was responsible for Cason Kellis's distasteful behavior, but he was sorry, nonetheless, that Emma had to deal with it.

"Maybe I should walk up to him the next time he shows up out here and tell him that I have no fricking idea whether the inventory number is right. Or, for that matter, whether the client's financial statements are materially accurate." Nelson paused as she began choking back tears. "Maybe I should also admit to him that I feel like I am way over my head on this audit and that I wasn't prepared to supervise the field work for a client as large as BRIC."

Bishop was long past the point of wanting to change the subject. As he sat there trying to come up with a humorous quip to lighten the moment, Nelson decided to maintain the heavy tone of the conversation.

"Since this is true confessions time, I might as well admit that I lied to you back in November or December when I told you that John Kelly and I were no longer seeing each other. We kept seeing each other until three weeks ago." Nelson blurted out the confession without looking at Bishop. "It wasn't working out, so we mutually decided to break up." Nelson intercepted Bishop's gaze. "Like I said before, I really appreciate your not telling anyone about John and me, especially Jim Wilmeth or Cason Kellis."

"No problem, Emma. I mean, I don't see that as any big deal."

"As much time as we spend on our jobs, Michael, there's not much chance to meet anyone except someone in our office or someone who works with one of our clients."

Bishop sensed that Nelson was about to unload another personal confession on him—and she was.

"I might as well leave here tonight with a totally clean conscience. Last year, a few weeks after the BRIC audit was finished, Bud Wallace called and asked me to go to dinner with him. I wasn't sure that I was going to be back on the BRIC audit team this year, so I went out with him a couple of times. Well, that was a stupid decision. He wound up being a real jerk. And now, as you well know, it is very uncomfortable for me to discuss anything with him or even to be in the same room with him."

Bishop nodded reassuringly as he struggled to maintain eye contact with Nelson.

"Sorry to ask, but that's another secret that I hope we can keep between the two of us. I know it's not exactly kosher to go out with someone in a client's accounting department. Although, I'm not sure exactly what the firm's rules are."

"Sure Emma. Don't worry about it."

This was the point in a heart-to-heart talk where the listening party was supposed to unload one or more of his or her personal issues or private concerns on the other party. Bishop would have none of that. Instead, he placed a cold slice of pizza on his plate signaling that he hoped the tell-all segment of their dinner date was over.

"By the way, has Bud Wallace said anything to you about that?" Nelson asked with a grimace.

Instead of verbally responding, Bishop took a bite of his sausage pizza and then shook his head sideways to indicate that Wallace had not mentioned the brief fling to him.

Michael Bishop was surprised to learn that his second meeting with the FBI would also be in the cavernous suburban mall where he had met the three agents six days earlier. It made him wonder what other familiar locations were favored FBI meeting places.

That Friday afternoon when Bishop walked into the small meeting room hidden on the mall's third floor, four men, including the three FBI agents who he had previously met, and one lady were sitting around the rickety dinette table in the middle of the room. The fourth man, who was in his mid-forties and dressed in a three-piece suit, didn't wait for one of the three agents to introduce him.

"Hello Michael. I am with the FBI's Washington, D.C., office. You can call me Irv." Similar to the other agents, Irv had a firm handshake, an intense gaze, and was engulfed in an unnerving aura of self-assuredness.

"This is Carol. She is with the D.C. office of the Securities and Exchange Commission." Carol was an attractive lady also in her mid-forties and, like Irv, was dressed in business attire—the three FBI agents who Bishop already knew were dressed casually in jeans as was the lookout agent who arrived a few minutes later. Bishop was not introduced to that individual who was in his mid-twenties and was easily the youngest of the agents.

"I know that the three agents here informed you of the seriousness of the situation in which you now find yourself, Michael. I want to reinforce that. This is a gravely serious matter, but we have complete confidence in you. Otherwise, you wouldn't be here today and we wouldn't be asking you to cooperate with us. Again, every word said today must be held in strictest confidentiality."

Irv stared at Bishop for several moments until the audit senior recognized that the FBI agent wanted a verbal acknowledgement of his previous statement.

"Yes. I understand."

"Michael, this week we have had two extended meetings in D.C. about this matter. Yesterday, we reached a decision. Our primary objective must be to obtain information about this secret organization that we refer to as the Agency. This organization's growing scope and power has the ability to disrupt our nation's stock markets. It is imperative that we somehow cripple and eventually destroy this organization. But we understand that goal may take years to achieve and will require us to expend considerable resources and sometimes force us to make decisions that have unfortunate consequences for innocent third parties."

The more Irv spoke and the more solemn he became, the more Bishop realized that his life had likely changed forever.

"We have decided that we want you to do exactly what Bud Wallace has asked you to do. By allowing the Agency's plan to succeed, that is, by allowing the organization to profit from the public disclosure of BRIC Industries' poor financial results, we believe that we may be able to identify several dozen individuals who are involved with that organization in some capacity, to identify key bank

accounts being used by the conspirators, and to better understand how the conspirators organize and carry out their schemes and distribute the profits from
them ex post. That is a distasteful decision for a number of reasons, not the least
of which is the fact that the organization stands to make tens of millions of dollars from this scam or the fact that the dishonest BRIC executives may not be
held accountable for their misconduct."

Irv paused to make sure that Bishop focused on the next point he was about
to make. "We have to look at this from a greater good perspective. Allowing the
Agency's plan to succeed should prove to be a tremendous benefit to every U.S.
citizen by providing us with crucial information about the organization."

For the next 30 minutes, or so, Irv, with occasional input from Jake and
Wayne, prepared Bishop for his James Bond-like, double-agent role over the following three weeks. The FBI agents hoped and actually expected that Bud Wallace's plan would work. They believed that after Wallace revealed the large
inventory misstatement, Cason Kellis would insist that Suzanne Jennings significantly reduce the fourth-quarter earnings number that she wanted to report.
BRIC's disclosure of the significant earnings shortfall for the fourth quarter and
the poor earnings forecast for the first quarter of the new year would send the
company's stock price into a free fall and allow the Agency to close out its short
positions at a huge profit.

If Kellis succumbed to pressure from Suzanne Jennings and BRIC's two other
senior executives and began cooperating with them to conceal the company's
poor earnings for the fourth quarter, someone would have to intercede. Hopefully, Nelson or Wilmeth would step up and confront Kellis and insist that BRIC's
fourth-quarter earnings had to be reduced. The FBI agents thought that was unlikely given what they had learned of those two individuals from Bishop and
other sources. Irv wanted Bishop, if at all possible, to avoid becoming directly
involved in ensuring the success of Bud Wallace's plan because that would likely
mean the end of his career in public accounting.

"What we would like you to do, Michael, is to remain employed with your firm
while, at the same time, secretly joining the Agency. To date, we have been un-
successful in our efforts to infiltrate the organization. But we think that there is
at least a reasonable chance that we could get you inside. Over a period of time,
you could feed us information that might help us destroy the Agency."

Bishop sat silently, along with everyone else in the room, after Irv dropped his
bombshell. Bishop had expected his life to change dramatically but not that dramatically. He wasn't sure what to say, what to think. Inwardly, his pulse was racing and his thoughts were spinning out of control; outwardly, he remained calm
and composed. Finally, after steadying himself, he spoke.

"What exactly do you have in mind for me?"

Irv explained to Bishop that they had devised a plan that might be successful in getting him accepted into the Agency. They wanted Bishop to approach Wallace privately. Bishop would tell the accounting manager that he had learned his true identity and was aware of his criminal background. Bishop would then reveal that he suspected Wallace intended to benefit from the negative earnings report for BRIC Industries by shorting the company's stock and then covering those positions after the poor earnings data were announced. At that point, Bishop would insist that Wallace pay him a sizable portion of the stock market gain that would be produced by the scam.

The FBI expected that Wallace would communicate with his contacts within the Agency and arrange another meeting between Bishop and members of the organization—the FBI was certain that "Charles" and "Zed," Wallace's alleged attorneys, were involved with the Agency. At that meeting, Bishop would present his demands. The FBI believed that the conspirators would not hesitate to pay Bishop a substantial sum given the huge profit the organization would earn— and the comparable loss that it would avoid—if BRIC's stock price plummeted.

Near the end of the meeting with the members of the Agency, Bishop would point out that in his role as an auditor of a Big Four accounting firm he routinely had access to crucial inside information for large public companies. He would then propose that by working together they could use that information to earn significant stock market gains on those companies' publicly-traded securities.

Irv told Bishop that he was not to suggest, in any way, that he was aware of the Agency. Instead, Bishop was to make it appear as if he thought he was dealing with a group of small-time con artists intending to make a quick profit in the stock market—that would be consistent with what Bishop had learned of Wallace's background. Irv went on to explain that the Agency often relied on individuals such as Wallace to make "scores" on specific stocks. But individuals with prior criminal records were not accepted as members of the organization. Instead, the Agency recruited only "straight-laced" professionals, including corporate attorneys, officers of stock registrar companies, executives of brokerage firms, securities analysts, and independent auditors. In fact, the FBI was convinced that independent auditors, including some audit partners, were a frequent source of inside information for the Agency.

If the BRIC case went as planned and Bishop convinced the Agency that he had the proper disposition, steady nerves, and resolve to participate in insider trading scams, the FBI hoped that he would eventually become a full-fledged member of the organization. Bishop would remain with his Big Four employer but would serve as an informant for the FBI while he consorted with the Agency.

"Michael, if you cooperate with us and are able to join the Agency, obviously your life is going to change. There is no doubt that your personal safety may be an issue, but, to date, we have no indication that the Agency resorts to physical violence. These men and women are from professional walks of life. They realize that if they were ever convicted of violating the federal securities laws, their prison sentences would be a fraction of what they would receive if they were convicted of a violent crime."

Despite the context in which the term was used, the word "violent" reverberated loudly in Bishop's mind.

"We know all about you and your background. Your personality and overall demeanor make you perfectly suited to work with us as does the fact that you do not have a large network of friends and family members. There is no doubt in our minds that, after thoroughly investigating you, senior members of the Agency would reach the same conclusion concerning your usefulness to their organization. And trust me. The Agency will thoroughly investigate you before considering you as a member."

The small room fell silent for several moments as Bishop sat contemplating his life, his future. Then, for the first time, Carol, the SEC official, spoke.

"Michael, you have been hearing from the FBI. Let me give you my perspective as a representative of the SEC. We are all convinced that this organization is involved in insider trading on a massive scale that is systematic and meticulously orchestrated. These individuals seek out and then compensate corporate insiders who can provide inside information that is not available to other investors. And then, they act on that information. In some cases, these schemes go on for years. We are convinced that this organization poses one of the largest threats, if not the largest threat, to the proper functioning of our nation's capital markets. In the current age of high technology, these criminals are not only extremely effective and efficient but also extremely elusive. To protect the integrity of the markets and literally to protect and promote the American way of life, we need individuals such as you to step up and help us."

The articulate and forceful lady paused momentarily before continuing. "Michael. You happen to be in a position in which you can help us tremendously. We understand that what we are asking you to do will disrupt your entire life, both personally and professionally. But we need you. Your country needs you."

Bishop leaned back in his chair after absorbing the forceful words and began doing the mental calculus for the extraordinary situation facing him. That calculus was not challenging.

In reality, Bishop didn't have a choice. The feds had already decided that he was perfectly suited to help them accomplish their goals and they were not going to accept "No" for an answer. He had forfeited the right to refuse to cooperate when he had agreed to go along with Wallace's plan. Instead of having free will to make his own choice in the matter, Bishop felt like a pawn, a powerless role player who would be forced to take orders from someone else. It was a role that he had become all too familiar with in public accounting over the previous few years.

As he slowly nodded his head to indicate that he would cooperate with the feds, Bishop realized and accepted the fact that he wouldn't be returning to his monotonous, humdrum, but safe and comforting lifestyle. Instead, adventure land awaited him. He resolved to make the best of it.

Chapter 15

Tuesday, February 4

"Hey, Bud."

Bud Wallace was surprised when he looked up and saw Michael Bishop standing at his door.

"What's up?"

"Do you have some time to meet with me later this afternoon?"

"Sure. Sure thing," Wallace replied. "How much time do you need?"

"I think thirty minutes should be enough. It's about two now. What about four-thirty?"

"Okay. You want to meet here in my office, or would you prefer that we find somewhere else that is a little quieter?"

"No, your office is fine." Bishop stepped forward and quietly added, "But I want a closed-door session with you."

The broad smile on Wallace's face faded away and was replaced by a concerned look that signaled both curiosity and anxiety.

Wallace cleared his throat and then muttered, "Okay," as Bishop turned and walked away.

Before his impending showdown with Bud Wallace, Michael Bishop met with Becky Linton and reviewed the exceptions noted by BRIC customers on returned receivables confirmations. Nearly 30 percent of the BRIC customers that had been mailed positive confirmation requests reported at least one disputed amount, while 25 percent of the customers that had been mailed negative confirmation requests disagreed with the balances reported for their accounts. Those were much higher exception rates than normal given Bishop's prior experience.

The confirmation exceptions ran the gamut. Although few in number, the most troubling exceptions involved a statement by the given customer something to the effect of, "We never received these goods." To help the customers confirm their year-end balances, the auditors had included with each positive confirmation request a detailed statement listing the charges that made up the given balance. No such statement was included with the negative confirmation requests.

Bishop told Linton to prepare a list of the confirmations that included exceptions for goods that the given customers had allegedly not received and then to ask one of BRIC's internal auditors to obtain copies of the bills of lading and other documentation for those transactions. He suggested that she wait a "week or so" before giving that list to the internal auditors. When Linton appeared puzzled by his suggestion, Bishop told her that, "Confirmations will continue to dribble in for a while. So, you should wait until all of the returned confirmations are available to make sure that the list is complete." In fact, because the sales were likely fraudulent, Bishop wanted to delay a thorough investigation of them. By the time it became evident that the sales were bogus, he hoped that Bud Wallace would have revealed the huge overstatement of BRIC's inventory. At that point, bringing the fraudulent sales to Cason Kellis's attention would only add to the firestorm of controversy on the BRIC audit rather than being the triggering mechanism for it.

Timing differences accounted for the largest number of reported exceptions on returned receivables confirmations. Two-thirds of these contested charges appeared to be for valid December sales; the customers had challenged those charges because the goods had not been received until after December 31. The goods in question had been shipped with terms of FOB shipping point on or before December 31 but delivered to the given customers after December 31—the shipping documents for these items confirmed that the goods had left the BRIC shipping dock by December 31. There was no question that the remaining exceptions due to timing differences involved sales that had been improperly recorded. These items were for goods that had not been shipped until January 1 or 2, which meant that BRIC should not have billed them to the customers until the new fiscal year.

For the first set of exceptions due to timing differences, Bishop instructed Linton to attempt to determine what proportion of those exceptions were due to BRIC's shipping-to-the-yard practice that it had ramped up during the final two weeks of the fiscal year. Bishop also told Linton to develop an estimate of the dollar amount of year-end receivables for the year under audit and the previous year that were due to the shipping-to-the-yard sales. He asked her to document that difference in her work papers and to prepare a proposed adjusting entry for that amount. Bishop also told Linton to estimate the amount of year-end receivables due to credit sales made during the first few days of January that had been recorded in December and to do the same for the previous year and to propose an adjusting entry for the difference between those two amounts as well. Bishop suggested that Linton wait for late-arriving confirmations before she tackled the job of developing the audit adjustments for the two types of timing differences.

The next most common type of exception in returned confirmations involved improper computation of trade discounts—in each case, the trade discount had been understated. BRIC had a multi-tiered trade discount structure. Highest volume customers were entitled to as much as a 25 percent trade discount, while the minimum trade discount was 10 percent. BRIC's customers had also been granted the new "seasonal" discount of 5 percent for any purchases they made in December. Because BRIC's billing software automatically calculated the dollar amount of each trade discount, Bishop suspected that this was a systematic error that likely affected a significant number of receivable accounts. He told Linton to review a sample of the confirmations returned without any exceptions to determine whether some customers had failed to detect billing overstatements due to improperly computed trade discounts.

Bishop couldn't recall whether Paula Henderson's crew had tested trade discounts and, if so, the results of those tests. The electronic files containing the internal control work papers were not available to Bishop or Nelson—Bishop had never been on an audit where the internal control work papers were not readily available during the performance of the year-end audit tests. Jim Wilmeth had explained to Bishop several weeks earlier that Cason Kellis had decided not to make the internal control work papers available during the audit's year-end substantive tests because that would "Just slow down those tests."

Because Wilmeth was in the audit conference room, Bishop decided to make the short walk from Linton's workspace to the conference room to ask him about the trade discounts. Wilmeth had a large spreadsheet with the caption "Medicare Receivables" spread out before him when Bishop entered the conference room. When Bishop asked him whether the trade discounts had been tested by Henderson or her subordinates, the audit manager responded "I have no idea" without looking up from the spreadsheet.

Over the previous few days, Wilmeth had become increasingly withdrawn. Because the audit manager was obviously in no mood to offer advice regarding the trade discount issue, Bishop decided to handle the matter himself. Rather than investigating the issue immediately, Bishop told Linton to include a note in the electronic work paper file for receivables indicating that a member of the audit team should discuss the apparent trade discounts problem with the appropriate client personnel before the audit was completed. Bishop realized that Emma Nelson would discover that note when she reviewed those work papers. At that point, Nelson would have to decide how to address the issue.

As the supervising audit senior, Nelson would be responsible for the initial review of the receivables work papers—and the other work paper files as well. After Nelson completed the initial review of a set of work papers, the auditor who had prepared them would "clear" her review comments. The second and third rounds of review would be performed by Wilmeth and Kellis, respectively, while the final, "big picture" review or overview of those work papers would be the responsibility of the concurring partner, Karol Eliason.

The final problem that Bishop helped Linton tackle was the large number of positive confirmations that were not returned by BRIC customers. The non-response rate was excessive given Bishop's past experience. Because a second round of requests was producing only a modest number of returned confirmations, Bishop told Linton not to send out a third wave to customers who had failed to respond to the first two requests. Instead, Bishop suggested to Linton that she begin applying alternative procedures to the unconfirmed accounts. That suggestion prompted a fatigued sigh from Linton who, similar to Bishop, seldom expressed any emotion. Bishop then anticipated and answered Linton's next unasked question.

"I'm guessing that most of the charges included in the unconfirmed accounts will not have been paid by now, so checking for subsequent cash receipts will not be very helpful and will just eat up a lot of your time. What you should do is start pulling the shipping documents for the billed charges in each unconfirmed account. You will then need to review those documents to determine that the charges were proper."

Because Bishop knew that retrieving and examining the large number of shipping documents would add 15 to 20 hours to Linton's workload, he told her that one of the rookie staff accountants would be assigned to help her with that task. He also told her that he would include a footnote in future time reports indicating that unanticipated problems had caused a significant number of additional hours to be spent on accounts receivable. Similar to most staff accountants, Linton was very cognizant of the time budget for each account for which she had primary responsibility.

Bishop glanced at his wristwatch and was surprised to find that it was almost 4:30 p.m. After giving Linton a few additional instructions, Bishop collected his thoughts, reviewed his game plan, and then headed for his *High Noon* confrontation with Bud Wallace a/k/a Joe Wallace.

"Hi Michael," Wallace said cautiously as Bishop stepped into his office and closed the door behind him.

Bishop didn't respond. Instead, he sat down in one of the two chairs facing Wallace's desk. As he sat there in silence, Bishop slowly moved his eyes from the left wall of Wallace's office, to the center wall behind Wallace, and then to the wall to his right.

"What do you have in mind, Michael?" Wallace asked warily.

"Just wondering," Bishop responded as he leveled his eyes on Wallace.

"Wondering what?"

"Just wondering why you don't have your CPA certificate displayed on one of your walls."

"Just a personal preference, I—"

"Where is your certificate?" Bishop asked pointedly before Wallace had finished responding to his previous question.

"That's a strange question." The tone of Wallace's voice was no longer courteous and respectful.

"What's so strange about the question? Do you even have a CPA certificate?"

"The question is strange because it isn't your style to ask personal questions of anyone." Wallace ignored Bishop's second question as he leaned back in his chair and crossed his arms on his chest.

"I'm just surprised that you're not a CPA." Bishop mimicked Wallace by crossing his arms on his chest and leaning back in his chair. "Especially since you told me back in December that you were worried about having the state board yank your certificate."

Wallace's ruddy complexion was turning to pewter gray as he stared down Bishop.

"And you never struck me as a Florida kind of guy."

"That's ironic," Wallace countered immediately, "because you never struck me as a California kind of guy." Wallace's statement was intended to signal that he had access to information regarding the secretive auditor's personal background.

The attempt to unnerve Bishop did not have the intended effect because the FBI had warned him that the Agency would investigate his background.

By this point, Wallace was a different person. To Bishop, it was as if Wallace had taken off a mask and revealed his true persona. Wallace's happy-go-lucky, devil-may-care disposition had been replaced by a mean-spirited, self-centered temperament. Even his voice was suddenly different—considerably lower with a southern accent that was readily discernible.

"Here's my read on this situation," Bishop said as he returned Wallace's angry glare and prepared to deliver his carefully scripted and well rehearsed accusations. "You and your two buddies, or, should I say, 'attorneys,' have sold short a large number of BRIC shares. Once you force Jennings to issue a disappointing earnings report, you guys are going to close those open positions and make a barrel of money in the process. Most likely, you are going to clear a profit of at least several hundred thousand dollars, if not more. That is, if Kellis doesn't cave in to Jennings and torpedo your plans."

"Better be careful, big boy," Wallace said derisively. "You're skating on thin ice."

"Yeah, right. You're the one who's on thin ice, not me. A judge or jury is not going to show you any leniency after you copped that plea down in Florida. As a two-time loser, you would be taking an extended, all-expense paid vacation to Club Fed."

Bishop got to his feet and then turned toward the door, which caused Wallace to quickly ask, "What do you want?"

"It should be obvious what I want," Bishop said after turning back to face Wallace. "I want a cut."

Wallace whistled softly as he shook his head from side to side. "Damn, I underestimated you. All this time, I thought you were just some tight-lipped, undersocialized dolt. But you proved me wrong. You are one cold-blooded SOB."

"Not really," Bishop replied calmly. "I'm just a businessman. A businessman just like you."

When Wallace replied, there wasn't any hint of anger in his voice. "I'll need a couple of days to arrange a meeting. I'm not in charge. You'll have to sit down with my, uh, my associates."

"Is it just the three of you? You and Charles and Zed?" Bishop asked.

Wallace shifted his weight in his chair as he delayed responding for a few moments.

"Yeah. It's just the three of us."

Because Wallace was lying, Bishop made a mental note of his facial expression and body language. He realized that information might prove to be useful later.

"But, again, you have to give me a little time to contact the other two." Wallace's voice suggested that he wanted some degree of assurance from Bishop that he wouldn't blow the whistle on the stock scam before Wallace had a chance to arrange a meeting with his two conspirators.

Instead of assurance, Bishop left Wallace with ambivalence by shrugging his shoulders indifferently before he opened the door and left.

An hour later, Bishop was standing in the audit conference room next to Becky Linton as she thumbed through a computer printout.

"Excuse me Becky, could I speak to you for a couple of minutes down in the break room, Michael?" Wallace asked the question in his friendly "Bud Wallace" voice.

"Sure, Bud. Just a second. Becky, dog ear those accounts when you find them. Later, we can discuss them after you track down the information for the individual customers."

Bishop walked shoulder to shoulder with a smiling Wallace past a long line of desks occupied by accounting clerks on the way to the break room. As was his manner, Wallace joked with a couple of the clerks as he passed their desks. But, as soon as the two of them ducked into the break room, Wallace dropped his cheerful facade.

"Okay. I have the meeting set up on Thursday evening," Wallace began. "My buddies assumed that you would want to meet in a public place. So, I will be waiting for you in my car at the intersection of Boyd and Chautauqua at eight-thirty on Thursday night. You can follow me to the meeting place that they have chosen."

"I will meet you at nine-thirty at that intersection," Bishop replied without hesitation.

Wallace was clearly annoyed but eventually nodded in agreement.

"What did Bud Wallace want?" Emma Nelson asked as soon as Bishop returned to the audit conference room.

"Oh, he was a little concerned that Becky and I had been taking up too much of the receivables clerk's time with questions about the confirmation exceptions. You know, the cute little blonde named Teagan."

Because he had been concentrating on coming up with a believable lie, Bishop had let his guard down and thrown in the "cute little blonde" phrase, an expression that he would normally never use in speaking with Nelson.

"'Cute little blonde,' huh?" Nelson said playfully as she arched one eyebrow. "Wow, that's a first."

Bishop immediately changed the subject. "Have you printed that SEC disclosure checklist? I wanted to take a quick look at it. I need to give Kaimee something to do for the next two hours. She can probably take care of some of the legwork for you on that checklist."

"Yes, here it is," Nelson responded and then added coyly, "I guess you don't think any of your female coworkers qualify as 'cute.'"

Bishop ignored Nelson's comment and instead focused his attention on the checklist that she had handed him.

Later that evening, as they left the audit conference room shortly after 9 p.m., Nelson told Bishop that she had called Cason Kellis during the afternoon.

"This time, I made it very clear to him that we have major unresolved problems on the audit, Michael. But he didn't respond well. He told me verbatim that I was 'borrowing trouble.' And then he added, 'I promise you everything is going to be fine.'"

"That sounds like our audit partner," Bishop replied as he opened the door to the parking garage for Nelson.

"So, what should I do?"

"Well, what else can you do at this point, Emma? If he won't listen to you, you always have the option of dissociating yourself from the audit opinion that he issues."

"Oh yeah. That would really further my career with the firm."

"You know, there are worse things than failing to become an audit partner."

Bishop was being sincere with Nelson because he realized that she might very well be one of the casualties of the forthcoming debacle.

Nelson opened the door to her new Mercedes that was a Christmas gift from her parents. "I know it wouldn't be a tragedy, Michael, okay? I'm not that shallow." After she slipped behind the wheel of her midnight blue sports coupe, Nelson added, "But ... it is what I want."

Chapter 16

Thursday, February 6

Michael Bishop was physically and mentally exhausted as he walked out of the audit conference room and flipped off the lights at 9:15 p.m. The enormous amount of overtime that he was working on the BRIC audit and the insidious and ever present stress imposed on him by his two new roles of fraud conspirator and FBI informant were taking a toll. As he prepared to rendezvous with Bud Wallace & Co., he knew that he had to be mentally sharp. Before leaving the ninth floor of the BRIC headquarters building, he stopped in a restroom and doused his face repeatedly with handfuls of cold water.

Bishop realized that working 75-80 hours per week was grossly inefficient and dysfunctional for the BRIC audit team. Team members had reached and passed the point of diminishing returns. Productivity, mental acuity, and one's professionalism began to erode at some point and Bishop knew that point was in the rearview mirror when it came to the members of the BRIC audit team. Even Emma Nelson had begun complaining of the exorbitant number of hours that she was working on the engagement.

The audit team had received some good news the day before. Cason Kellis had sent the BRIC auditors an email telling them that they would each receive an extra 40 hours of vacation time to compensate them, marginally, for the excessive overtime they were working. The abrupt resignation of the two rookie staff accountants the previous week had likely prompted Kellis to make that modest concession to his troops.

———————

Bishop cracked open the door to the parking garage that was adjacent to the BRIC headquarters building and surveyed the floor where his car was parked. Although he knew that FBI agents were tracking him with state-of-the-art surveillance technology, he wasn't certain they could ensure his safety in the parking structure. Bishop hoped that the meeting with Wallace and his associates would go smoothly. It was imperative for him to get back to his apartment and try to get some sleep since he had slept no more than a few hours the night before. Despite all of the drama in his life, at this point sleep was his number one priority.

After Bishop spotted Wallace's sports car sitting in a vacant parking lot near the intersection where they had agreed to meet, he flashed his headlights, signaling Wallace to pull in front of him on the four-lane city street. It was freezing outside, but Bishop's driver side window was halfway open and funneling an Arctic blast into his car. Bishop was doing everything he could to ensure that he could hold his own in the coming battle of wits.

Wallace's left-hand turn signal was flashing as they approached a seedy bowling alley on the fringe of the downtown business district. The bowling alley's nearby neighbors included an abandoned warehouse, an abandoned metro bus station, and a drive-by liquor store with windows guarded by steel bars.

Bishop was not wearing a wire; the FBI didn't want to take the chance that he would be searched either by hand or electronically. Although he had a cell phone with a microphone that could be remotely activated, Bishop had been instructed to leave it in the car as well for the same reason.

The FBI agents had warned Bishop that despite being stationed somewhere nearby, there was less than a 50-50 chance that they would be able to get near enough to record his conversations. Even if the agents could get close enough to record those conversations, it was possible that the Agency would use counter surveillance equipment to "jam" their listening devices. The agents had also told Bishop that wherever the meeting took place there would almost certainly be other Agency members present in addition to Charles and Zed—either overtly or covertly or both. In fact, the FBI agents hoped that other members of the organization would be present because they would be using video surveillance equipment and facial recognition software to identify anyone who was present at the meeting place when they subsequently left.

Bishop followed several feet behind Wallace as the accounting manager led him through the dimly-lit interior of the decrepit bowling alley. Only a handful of the 20 or so lanes were being used and only three of the two dozen or so tables in the dining room that lay adjacent to the snack bar were occupied. One of those tables was in the far corner of the dining room, easily out of earshot of the other patrons. Sitting at the table were three men, not two. It was the first of many surprises that Bishop was about to experience.

"You have met Charles and Zed before," Wallace said apprehensively to Bishop as he motioned to his two confederates who Bishop had previously encountered. Neither of the two men stirred or smiled or in any way acknowledged Bishop's presence. Wallace then turned to the third man seated at the table. "This is ..."

"Michael, my name is Malachi. You can call me Mal." As Bishop stared at the third man who had stood and extended his right hand, a fleeting thought raced through his mind, namely, why Charles had been deprived of a cool Old Testament name.

Bishop hesitated momentarily before reaching out and shaking Mal's hand. Similar to Charles and Zed, Mal was wearing dress slacks, an open-collar shirt, and a pullover sweater. The men's heavy winter coats were piled on an adjacent table.

Before Bishop made a move to sit down, he turned to Wallace, "You said there were only three of you involved in this."

Wallace didn't face Bishop or respond to his question.

"Michael," Mal began in an apologetic tone, "I want to take responsibility for my presence here. Joe, I mean, for your purposes, Bud, didn't know that I was going to be here. In fact, he and I have never met before."

"Joe," Mal said addressing Wallace, "you can leave now. Thanks for bringing Michael."

Wallace was obviously surprised. He looked first at Zed and then at Charles. After a few moments, Charles nodded in the direction of the bowling alley's front door. Wallace stood silently for a few more moments before turning and plodding away.

As Wallace walked away, Bishop grudgingly took off his coat and sat down at the table.

"Again, I apologize," Mal said as he placed his elbows on the table, clasped his hands together, and leaned slightly forward. "I decided to join Charles and Zed here tonight just a few hours ago."

"Maybe so, but Wallace had told me … he had assured me, that there were just three people involved in this … this situation. Now I'm wondering what is going on." Bishop knew that anger was the appropriate emotion for him to display. He just hoped that his feigned anger passed for the real thing.

"Before you leave here tonight, Michael, you will have a better understanding, hopefully, a complete understanding of this 'situation,' to use your word, and all the surrounding circumstances," Mal replied.

Bishop was surprised by Mal's appearance and manner. He expected that an apparently senior member of a professional crime syndicate would be smooth, articulate, and personally impressive. Mal was none of those. Unlike the squared-jaw, athletic, and handsome Charles and Zed, Mal was in his early fifties, gray and balding, with a modest middle-aged paunch hanging over his belt. He better fit the role of the manager of a small grocery store, a postal clerk, or a Sunday school teacher than a big-time crook.

"Michael, the three of us here represent just a small fraction of a large organization," Mal said quietly. "This organization has existed for quite some time and it becomes larger each year. We view ourselves primarily as a public service organization."

Bishop laughed under his breath and looked away. Surely that was the appropriate reaction to such a seemingly outlandish statement, he thought to himself. To appear authentic, Bishop also knew that his timing had to be flawless.

"I understand your reaction," Mal said in response to Bishop's apparent disdain. "Yes, we do engage in insider trading. Yes, we profit from that trading. But we view what we are doing as necessary to make our nation's capital markets function better. And more fairly for everyone."

Bishop wondered how an organization that stole from millions of small-time investors could have the audacity to claim that it was serving the public interest. He also wondered why Mal would make such a statement when he, Bishop, was there to join a criminal enterprise not a public service organization.

"There is no doubt that many of us joined this organization to make a good living by engaging in insider trading, which is clearly considered an illegal activity by law enforcement authorities and the courts. In fact, you're here tonight for a similar reason."

As Mal paused briefly, his two robotic associates kept their eyes riveted on Bishop. Once again, they apparently had been charged with the responsibility of gauging Bishop's every reaction to what he was being told.

"But, over time, this organization has evolved and changed," Mal continued. "The leaders of the organization, and that includes me, are no longer self-interested mercenaries. We know that Corporate America is corrupt. We know that billions and billions of dollars are being drained out of our economy every year by selfless and soulless criminals. We know that corporate executives, Congressmen, federal judges, celebrities, and, yes, even partners of Big Four firms are profiting enormously from this corruption." Each time that Mal used the phrase "We know" he jammed the end of his right index finger into the open palm of his left hand. "And who suffers from that corruption? Honest, everyday folks who spend their lives working to provide a decent livelihood for themselves and their families. Small business owners in Birmingham, Alabama, oil field workers in Oklahoma, and ... elementary school teachers in Seal Beach, California."

Bishop, who had been feigning disinterest by gazing at three foulmouthed teenagers bowling to his right, turned and faced Mal after he made the oblique reference to his mother.

"Michael, this cancer is damaging our entire economic system and is threatening to destroy it. We don't want that to happen. We want to be part of the solution rather than being part of the problem."

Mal studied Bishop's face for several moments before he spoke again.

"You are not going to be paid a dime for cooperating with us. We are not going to contribute to causing a fine young man to become a criminal. We know you, we know who you are. You have experienced tragedy and, as a result, maybe you have lost your bearings. That is not a sufficient reason for you to throw everything away and make a horrible decision that will lead you down a path that you don't want to go."

Bishop looked away. He didn't need or want to be psychoanalyzed again.

"Your mother struggles financially, Michael," Mal said quietly in an earnest tone. "If you cooperate with us, we will make arrangements to pay off the mortgage on her small home. We will also arrange to have your sister receive a four-year scholarship to the campus of her choice in the University of California system."

Suddenly, Bishop once more felt physically and mentally exhausted. He also felt bewildered. He had prepared for a wide range of contingencies that might arise during this meeting. But the scenario that was unfolding was not one of them.

"What we want is for you to join our organization. We have a need for professional auditors with the major accounting firms to become a part of our organization. With your character, composure, and intellect, you would be a tremendous asset for us."

Over the next 20 minutes, Mal provided Bishop with a more in-depth understanding of his "organization." The great majority of the information that Mal provided was consistent with what the FBI had told Bishop about the Agency.

Mal told Bishop that his organization identified companies whose executives were suspected of misrepresenting their reported earnings and then obtained information from corporate insiders or other parties to confirm that suspicion. After short selling a "modest volume" of such a company's stock, the organization then "punished" the company and their dishonest executives by driving down or "correcting" the company's stock price. The methods used for that purpose included sabotaging the company's accounting scam, coercing the executives involved to voluntarily reveal the scam, or compelling those executives to record bogus write-offs or other phony accounting adjustments that corrected their company's previously overstated earnings. The latter method was the most common and preferred strategy used by the Agency since it was less likely to prompt an investigation by the SEC or the filing of class-action lawsuits, either of which could potentially focus unwanted attention on the short-selling activity in the given stock.

Absent the actions of his organization, Mal insisted that numerous large-scale accounting scams would have gone on indefinitely. By short-circuiting those scams, the organization had minimized the damage that they did to investors and to the overall integrity of the capital markets.

Mal justified the insider trading profits earned by his organization by explaining that it had "significant" expenses that had to be covered. Those expenses included the "distasteful" bribes that had to be paid to "corporate informants" such as Joe Wallace. He then assured Bishop that individuals such as Wallace were purely "one-offs" who were paid for inside information regarding a given company but who would never be considered for membership in their organization.

The organization's expenses also included the "salaries" of its members, Mal readily admitted. Since many of those members worked full-time in "this line of business," they had to forego other opportunities to earn a livelihood. Mal maintained that the salaries distributed to the organization's members were not excessive and that they did not live like "rock stars." Even the organization's most highly compensated members, including himself, only enjoyed "comfortable upper-middle class lifestyles."

The only point at which Mal became overtly emotional was when he discussed his organization's principal antagonists. Surprisingly to Bishop, those antagonists were not law enforcement or regulatory agencies. In Mal's words, "Those men and women are just doing their jobs. They are well-intentioned although their efforts are misdirected."

Instead, the organization's principal enemies were corrupt corporate executives who manipulated their companies' reported financial data and a few large hedge funds that routinely earned massive trading profits at the expense of other investors. Mal argued that, unlike his organization, the "rogue" hedge funds had no redeeming value. Those hedge funds paid dishonest corporate executives for inside information that they then traded on to earn huge stock market gains. The rogue hedge funds also disrupted corporate financial reporting and the stock markets by distributing false inside information regarding publicly-owned companies that they then traded on to the detriment of honest investors.

Mal referred to hedge funds as "unregulated black boxes" that operated with "impunity." He insisted that law enforcement and regulatory authorities should focus their time and energy on investigating and prosecuting the rogue hedge funds and the corporate executives who conspired and cooperated with them. Mal also insisted that some of those funds were controlled by "international crime syndicates."

Near the end of his extended monologue, Mal also attacked the Big Four accounting firms that audit the great majority of large public companies. Mal suggested that his organization was necessary because the Big Four firms refused "to properly police" the financial reporting domain. "Your employer and the other major accounting firms have created a culture in which they are too concerned with lining their pockets with the huge fees paid to them by their clients to be objective financial detectives. In fact, when the big accounting firms uncover accounting frauds, they often look the other way rather than blow the whistle on those frauds."

By the end of Mal's speech, Bishop's head was throbbing. Suddenly, nothing seemed clear-cut in his mind and that included the central issue at hand, namely, the question of whether insider trading was improper. Bishop knew that insider trading was a controversial and hotly debated subject within the world of high finance and economics. Many reputable parties, including the famed economist and Nobel Prize winner Milton Friedman, had argued that insider trading predicated on truthful insider information should not be prohibited. According to Friedman and others, such insider trading would serve to quickly impound all relevant information into the prices of publicly traded securities, making the markets fairer for investors who didn't have the wherewithal to access such information.

Other proponents of legalizing "honest" insider trading had pointed out that in most economic markets either the buyer or seller has inside information that does not have to be shared with the other party to the transaction. So, why should corporate insiders who have access to such information and act on it be singled out for punishment?

Regardless of whether insider trading was justified in at least some circumstances, Bishop realized that the views expressed, and arguments made, by Mal were largely self-serving. He also recognized that much of what he had been told may have been abject lies or distortions of the truth.

One telltale red flag in Mal's story was his insistence that his organization only engaged in a "modest volume" of insider trading involving any one company. The FBI had told Bishop that there was a huge "overhang" of short positions in BRIC's stock that was apparently attributable to the Agency. If the Agency only had a modest volume of outstanding short positions in the company's stock, it seemed unlikely that the organization would take the risk of trying to persuade a member of the BRIC audit team to cooperate with a plan to force BRIC to report negative operating results.

As he sat there trying to solve the Rubik's Cube conundrum that he faced, Bishop realized that he had to "play along" with the Agency regardless.

"So, what exactly do you want me to do?" Bishop asked with as much intensity as he could muster.

"What we want you to do is to help ensure that the plan Joe Wallace has laid out for you is successful." Mal seemed more relaxed, most likely because he perceived that Bishop had decided to cooperate with him and his organization. "In a sense, Michael, you are insurance for us. If Kellis capitulates to pressure exerted on him by Jennings, he may simply choose to ignore the adverse inventory data that Wallace is going to reveal shortly before the date of the earnings press release. If that happens, then you will have to do whatever is necessary to make certain that BRIC records the appropriate adjustments for the overstated inventory. That might include somehow threatening to go to the managing partner of your office or another senior partner of your firm."

It was mind-boggling to Bishop that both the FBI and the Agency wanted him to do exactly the same thing.

"There is no doubt that there may be some unintended and adverse consequences for some innocent parties," Mal continued. "We don't care about Kellis. If he loses his job, all the better. If Jennings and her co-conspirators, meaning Hakes and Zimmer, are fired, all the better. But there may be negative fallout for individuals such as Miss Nelson." Mal paused to reinforce his next point. "You have to keep in mind that regardless of the negative consequences for any one person, it's the greater good that we are pursuing. We have one and only one goal and that is to make certain that BRIC's stock price collapses."

As soon as the last few words left Mal's mouth, Bishop could see him visibly recoil. Those words seem to convey that monetary issues were Mal's main concern rather than the "greater good" point of view that he had strenuously promoted.

"Of course, when that stock price goes down, then our primary objective will have been accomplished. By that, I mean that ... well ... that we will have short-circuited one more accounting fraud and ... and corrected the given company's stock price for the benefit of ... of other investors," Mal stumbled and stammered in his attempt to undo any damage done by his previous statement.

Bishop decided that he should divert attention from Mal's apparent misstep.

"I have a question. Do you think that all audit partners are crooks?" It wasn't the most artistic or relevant question, but it served Bishop's purpose.

"No, not at all. I didn't mean to leave you with that impression when I attacked your profession. The truth is that many Big Four audit partners are hard-working, honest, diligent professionals. But," Mal lightly pounded his right fist on the tabletop, "the greedy culture of the Big Four firms overwhelms those partners and often forces even them to capitulate to their big corporate clients."

Bishop acted as if he was satisfied by Mal's response. A few moments later, he glanced at his wristwatch, which prompted Mal to speak once more.

"Michael, can we rely on you? On your help?"

Bishop sat silently, suggesting that he was deep in thought and considering all of his options. When a seemingly appropriate period of time had elapsed, he responded.

"Yes. I will cooperate with you." Bishop took a calculated risk in an effort to make his decision appear more genuine. "I just wish you had been upfront with me from the very beginning."

"Michael, try to look at this problem from our perspective. We thought that it was best for Wallace to feed you that bogus story about his father because that story was much easier for you to process. If we had known how insightful you are, believe me, we would have been totally honest with you from the beginning."

Bishop thought that Mal's use and emphasis of the word "honest" was over-done. It made him suspect that Mal was being deceptive.

After an extended pause, Mal decided that his explanation had satisfied Bishop, so he changed the subject to signal that their meeting was almost over.

"Michael, understand that we are not going to contact you over the next few weeks unless it is necessary. If we do have to contact you, we will communicate with you through Joe Wallace."

Bishop acquiesced with a slight nod of his head.

"If this situation evolves as we think it will, we will not contact you again for at least three to five months. You have to be patient. By the time we contact you again, we will have made the arrangements to pay your mother's mortgage and to provide the scholarship for your sister that I previously described. Under-stand that neither of them will ever know of your role in either of those matters."

Chapter 17

Saturday, February 8

Michael Bishop wandered around the maze-like structure of the second floor searching for a door with a "Tanner R. White" nameplate. It was 7:24 a.m. on Saturday morning, February 8, and Bishop hoped to be in the audit conference room by 8 a.m. The day before, on Friday morning, he had made his routine stop at the 7-11 near his apartment at precisely 7:02 a.m.—the FBI had established a schedule of daily arrival times at the convenience store for Bishop. Those arrival times ranged from 6:55 a.m. to 7:12 a.m. The FBI didn't want Bishop to arrive at the same time each day because that might be a red flag if he was under surveillance.

Most mornings, the 7-11 stop was uneventful. Bishop would purchase a morning paper, a drink, and possibly a pastry and then head for BRIC's headquarters. Occasionally, though, he would be slipped a note by a fellow customer. The exchange always took place near the drink cooler in a blind spot hidden from the store's surveillance cameras. Friday morning, Bishop had been slipped a note that instructed him to meet with the FBI the following morning in the "Tanner R. White" office on the second floor of BRIC's headquarters building—the company's engineering department was housed on that floor.

Tanner White was no longer employed by BRIC or had been transferred to a larger, more luxurious office than the glorified master bedroom closet in which he had been previously stationed. Bishop didn't ask Jake how he had arranged a meeting in a vacant office in BRIC's headquarters building. The audit senior had quickly realized that he was on a strict need-to-know basis with the FBI: if he didn't need to know something, the FBI agents didn't tell him—and that was more than fine with him.

"Michael, we didn't get any usable audio from your meeting Thursday night," Jake said as he motioned Bishop to sit in a chair between himself and Wayne, the auditor-turned-FBI agent. Lee, the appointed stenographer for the troika, was sitting behind Tanner's former desk, prepared to pound away at the keyboard of his laptop computer. "But we got some great video. We were able to capture complete face shots of everyone who left the bowling alley that night before closing. We matched four of the face shots with individuals who we had previously caught on video."

Jake retrieved four 8 × 11 color photos from his satchel and laid them on the top of Tanner's desk. Two of the photos were of Charles and Zed. Bishop wasn't certain, but he believed the other two photos were of a couple of scraggly characters that had been bowling that night. The two men in their mid-twenties sported unkempt beards and were dressed in flannel shirts and faded blue jeans—the agents had instructed Bishop to make mental notes of any other patrons that he witnessed in the bowling alley that night.

Bishop picked Mal's photo out of a stack of color photos that the FBI had taken of the other individuals who had left the bowling alley following his meeting with the Agency representatives.

"Very good," Jake said enthusiastically after Bishop identified Mal's photo. "We will cross-check this guy's photo a second time against the large photo database that we have put together investigating the Agency. Maybe he will turn up somewhere."

For 25 minutes, Bishop provided the agents a blow-by-blow account of the bowling alley meeting with the help of two pages of notes that he had scribbled before falling asleep after he returned home to his apartment on Thursday evening. As they debriefed Bishop, Jake and Wayne reacted to several of the statements made by Mal.

"Man alive, these guys can spin quite a story. Either that or they are completely delusional," Jake commented after Bishop reported that Mal had used the phrase "public service organization" to describe the insider trading network to which he belonged.

"What crap," Wayne said with a boisterous laugh when Bishop reported that Mal lived a "comfortable upper-middle class" lifestyle. "He forgot to mention the yachts they have docked at St. Kitts and St. Lucia in the Caribbean and Malta in the Mediterranean."

Bishop wanted to ask Wayne if that was speculation on his part or whether the FBI had traced such assets to Agency members. But, on a need-to-know basis, Bishop didn't need to know, so he didn't ask.

At the conclusion of the debriefing, Jake and Wayne were elated.

"Michael, this is great. Who knows, this 'Mal' character may prove to be a big fish within the Agency," Jake said as he extended his right hand to Bishop. "You must have impressed these guys because I don't think they are blowing smoke. I think they really want you to join their organization."

Bishop was hoping that Jake or Wayne would comment on the Agency's promise to pay off his mother's mortgage and to arrange a four-year scholarship for his sister, but they didn't. Those promises had been floating around in Bishop's head since he left the bowling alley. Because the feds were allowing the Agency to make tens of millions of dollars on the BRIC insider trading scam, he hoped that his mother and sister would be allowed to benefit from the relatively paltry amounts that the Agency would pay on their behalf—assuming, of course, that the Agency actually made those payments, which Bishop realized was an enormous assumption.

As Bishop was preparing to leave, Jake told him to take mental notes of any unusual activity that he observed at BRIC's headquarters or elsewhere. If an emergency arose, Jake reminded Bishop to use the secure cell phone that he had been given previously to contact the FBI.

After returning to the audit conference room, Bishop gathered some notes he had written and went in search of Becky Linton. Over the previous week, while she was waiting for additional receivables confirmations to come in, Linton had completed her work on three of BRIC's accrued liabilities accounts: the warranty reserve, the reserve for hourly employee vacations, and the year-end accrued payroll for hourly employees. Linton's investigation of those three accounts had revealed some troubling red flags.

In the past, BRIC had recorded accrued warranty expense at the rate of 3.25 percent of annual sales. For the year under audit, that number had been reduced to 2.15 percent. When Linton asked the accounting clerk responsible for the warranty account why the accrual percentage had been reduced, the clerk responded that, "I don't know, but I will try to find out."

The BRIC audit program required Becky to perform reasonableness tests to provide a quick check on the material accuracy of the reserve for hourly employee vacations and the year-end accrued payroll for hourly employees. If the tests suggested that those amounts were reasonably accurate, no more testing was required by the audit program. Alternatively, if the expected balance yielded by a reasonableness test and the actual dollar amount for the given account were significantly different, then more testing—principally client inquiry and more detailed analytical procedures—would be necessary.

Linton's reasonableness tests for the two payroll-related liabilities were based upon two key factors: the average size of BRIC's workforce for the year under audit versus that of the previous year and changes in the union pay scale during the past year. For the accrued payroll account, Becky also compared the length of the "stub period" at year-end for the year under audit to that of the previous year. For both accrued liabilities, Becky's reasonableness tests suggested that they might be understated by as much as 20 percent. Because those understatements individually were not material relative to BRIC's pre-audit net income, Linton had decided that further testing of the accounts was unnecessary. Bishop intended to discuss that conclusion with her.

Another issue on Bishop's "to do" list was to ask Linton about some suspicious payments that she had uncovered while performing the search for unrecorded liabilities. On Monday, during one of Cason Kellis's frequent I-just-called-to-chat sessions with Emma Nelson, Nelson had told the audit partner that she and her audit team were facing major time constraints. Kellis had then suggested that Nelson "truncate some of the audit tests." When she pressed him for an example, he told her to shorten the test window for the search for unrecorded liabilities from six weeks to just the month of January.

Linton had compiled a list of 15 vendor payments made by BRIC during January that had not been recorded as liabilities (accounts payable) as of December 31. When she pulled the vouchers for those payments, the supporting documents suggested that the given transactions involved purchases made from vendors during December, meaning that year-end liabilities should have been booked for each of those transactions. Linton had briefly discussed those payments with the head accounts payable clerk. The accounts payable clerk had insisted that rather than being payments for December purchases that the given amounts were actually "customer deposits." According to Linton's translation of the clerk's explanation, when BRIC Industries reached its credit limit with certain large vendors the company was required to make advance payments or "deposits" with those vendors before any subsequent purchase transactions could be processed.

Bishop had worked with clients that were required to make advance payments to their vendors because they were high credit risks. However, in this case, the red, if not scarlet, flag was the information in the supporting vouchers for the disbursements. If Linton had correctly interpreted those vouchers, then the accounts payable clerk's explanation was not reasonable. In Bishop's mind, either the clerk was incompetent or she was attempting to obscure the true nature of the payments. After discussing the suspicious payments with Linton and examining himself the documents in question, Bishop planned to have Linton expand the search for unrecorded liabilities by lowering by 25 percent the cutoff threshold for identifying potential unrecorded liabilities at year-end.

The key issue that Bishop wanted to address with Linton was a "letter of inquiry" from the Environmental Protection Agency that she had discovered two days earlier while meeting with the head accounts payable clerk. While investigating that letter, Linton had found an internal BRIC memo that referred to an upcoming "show cause" hearing with EPA officials. Bishop had asked Linton to investigate the EPA matter on Friday and he planned to talk to her to find out what she had learned. The previous week, Emma Nelson had asked Bishop to complete the GAAP disclosure checklist. Bishop had interviewed several BRIC accounting employees — with the notable exception of Bud Wallace — while completing that checklist and none of them had mentioned the EPA matter when they were asked about potential loss contingencies that BRIC faced.

By this point in the audit, Bishop was spending most of his time helping Linton and the four rookie staff accountants resolve problems that they had uncovered in their assigned accounts. Nelson was doing the same with Coleman Jackson as he attempted to complete the inventory audit procedures. Nelson should have been reviewing work paper files for the most important client accounts but she couldn't since those files were not complete.

The open issues that remained for Linton's liability accounts were symptomatic of the status of the BRIC audit: there were loose ends everywhere. As the BRIC audit lurched clumsily toward its conclusion, Bishop knew that those loose ends could not be properly addressed and resolved before Wallace "accidentally" leaked the information regarding the huge inventory overstatement to the audit team—which was exactly what Bishop wanted.

Neither Kellis nor Wilmeth were apparently fazed by the troubling picture painted by the weekly progress reports and accompanying Gantt charts that Bishop submitted to them each week via Emma Nelson. Even a brief review of those documents would have revealed that the audit was nowhere near to being complete.

Despite being woefully behind schedule, the BRIC audit team had collected an impressive amount of audit evidence. Any objective party who reviewed that evidence could only reach one conclusion, namely, that BRIC's accounting records were not only incredibly sloppy but also replete with errors. If those errors were accumulated, there was no doubt in Bishop's mind that BRIC's pre-audit net income number of fifty-nine cents per share for the fourth quarter was grossly overstated.

"Michael, it's 8:39 p.m. on Saturday night and I am starving. How about we head to Curcio's and devour an entire Sicilian meatball pizza?" Emma Nelson asked as she and Michael Bishop sat alone in the audit conference room—Jim Wilmeth had "clocked-out" early, as usual.

"Let's see," Bishop said as he leaned back in his chair and gazed at the ceiling. "If we throw in the three slices of ciabatta bread that we normally eat with the house salad and the monstrous serving of tiramisu that we share to top off the meal, we are probably looking at between two thousand and twenty-five hundred calories … each. Right?"

"Wait a minute. Not only are you spoiling the highlight of my entire day, you are also explaining why my clothes no longer fit," Nelson responded with a weary laugh.

"What the heck," Bishop responded. "I say we go for it. If we expire from overwork, they can bring in a forklift to get us out of here."

Despite her many peccadilloes, Bishop had come to understand and to like Nelson. If one overlooked those peccadilloes—which included her overwrought concern with her personal appearance, her inability to treat her subordinates with a reasonable degree of civility, and her never-ending quest to promote her own self-interest—Emma Nelson was a decent human being. Bishop respected her hard-nosed, bulldog-like resilience and tenacity. For a beautiful young lady whose hair was always perfectly coiffed and whose nails were always immaculately manicured, she could work a Teamster under the table.

Bishop considered himself an expert in "reading" people. But there was a sizable blind spot in his sixth sense, namely, his inability to read the romantic interests of women. He was considerably less than certain, but it seemed that Nelson had developed a personal interest in him that extended beyond their working relationship. In terms of that working relationship, there was no doubt in Bishop's mind that Nelson's opinion of him had evolved over the previous four months. She no longer viewed him as a slacker or even as her subordinate. Over the same time span, Nelson's opinion of Cason Kellis had changed even more dramatically. Not only did she view the audit partner as a fourth-stage lecher, it was obvious that she also had come to doubt his professional judgment and competence.

Chapter 18

Friday, February 14

7:45 a.m.

As he stepped into a restroom on the ninth floor of BRIC's headquarters building, Michael Bishop retrieved the folded note from his front pocket that he had been given by a frail grandfather at his local 7-11. In the note, Jake instructed Bishop to go to Tanner White's office on Sunday, February 16, at 7:30 a.m. By this time, Bishop had been given his own key to Tanner's office. After re-reading the brief note, Bishop ripped it apart and sent it on its journey through the metro sewer system.

───────────

The exhausted staff accountants on the BRIC audit team were counting the days down to February 24. Once the client issued its earnings press release on that day, the audit team would shift into the "end game" of the engagement. That phase of the BRIC audit would involve, among other tasks, clearing the remaining review comments in the work paper files, finalizing the summary memos for the major accounts, a final scan of the accounting records for any unusual post-year-end transactions, and a final search for significant subsequent events. Before the audit team members moved on to their next assignments, Emma Nelson would prepare a performance appraisal for each of them and schedule one-on-one sessions to discuss those reports.

Earlier in the week, Cason Kellis, who continued to be seemingly oblivious to the fact that the BRIC audit was hugely behind schedule, had sent out an upbeat email to audit team members informing them that as of Monday, February 24, the maximum work week for the BRIC engagement would nosedive to no more than 55 hours. He added that each of them could expect to return to a workload of 45 hours within two to three weeks once they were released from the BRIC engagement. He finished off the email by indicating that he had never worked with a more dedicated and professional audit team and that he was extremely proud of the manner in which they had dealt with the "unforeseen challenges posed by this audit."

Kellis's email did not mention the two rookie accountants who had walked out on the engagement, the fact that other team members had threatened to mutiny, or that the audit manager on the job had morphed into a bitter recluse who avoided his subordinates and spent most of his time working on another engagement.

A few minutes after sending out the email, Kellis added a brief postscript informing the audit team members that under no circumstances were they to work past 5 p.m. on Friday, which was Valentine's Day. "I don't want to be responsible for preventing any of you from ending the week without a romantic tryst ... and, I want you to enjoy that tryst at the firm's expense!" The team members were instructed to submit the dinner bill for their Valentine outing with their next monthly expense report.

8:55 a.m.

"Michael, is Becky making progress on wrapping up the receivables account?" Emma Nelson asked as Michael Bishop walked into the audit conference room following a meeting with Becky Linton. The two audit seniors had the room to themselves—Jim Wilmeth had sent Nelson a brief email at 8 a.m. letting her know that he would be spending the morning at the practice office with Cason Kellis.

"She is making progress, but I wouldn't say that the end is in sight," Bishop replied as he sat down at the conference table across from Nelson.

"So, we don't know when she will wrap up receivables?"

"The problem, Emma, is that in addition to trying to wrap up the receivables account, Becky is fighting fires all over the place. She still hasn't quite completed the search for unrecorded liabilities—I've asked Kaimee to spend today helping her on that test; she and I need to find some time to sit down and discuss the accrued payroll liabilities numbers; and a client clerk has been dragging her feet producing the documents that Becky has requested regarding that EPA investigation."

"Becky has to become more assertive with the client's clerks and other personnel," Nelson replied. "It's tough to be assertive, though, when you can't even make eye contact with the person you're speaking with."

"Yeah, I guess that's true." Bishop recognized that Linton had certain limitations, but he didn't think it was appropriate to criticize such a reliable and industrious subordinate.

"I hate to say this, Michael, but I think that beginning tomorrow, after our big Valentine's Day 'vacation' of three or four hours, we may need to require everyone to put in twelve chargeable hours each day. Kellis will be showing up out here late next week to review the work papers for all of the major accounts before he meets with Suzanne Jennings." Nelson paused as she checked a text message on her cell phone.

Cason Kellis had told Nelson a few days earlier that considerable time could be saved by not having Jim Wilmeth involved in the review of the audit work papers. So, once Nelson's review comments were cleared by her subordinates, the work papers would be ready for Kellis. The audit partner indicated that he could complete his review in two days or less—which meant to Bishop that Kellis intended to fly through the work papers at a record pace. Bishop also suspected that Kellis would ignore his policy of requiring the work papers to be "picture perfect" since BRIC's work papers would be slipshod, to say the least.

"That was my Mom. She wants to know what I'm doing for Valentine's Day," Nelson said with a laugh as she put away her phone. "Anyway, we need to somehow start getting some degree of closure on the major accounts even if it means just documenting the unresolved issues in the work papers and then moving on." There was a tone of fatalistic resignation in Nelson's voice. "That will allow me to do a quick, down and dirty review of those accounts and then turn them back to the staff accountants. I'll insist that they spend only a token amount of time and effort clearing my comments."

Bishop didn't respond to Nelson's decision to turn the work paper files over to Kellis incomplete. Instead, he focused on the secondary workload issue that she had raised.

"Well, if you want me to, I will tell the staff accountants that they will need to buckle down and extend their workdays by one hour."

During the past week, Bishop had noticed for the first time a dramatic change in Nelson's attitude toward the BRIC audit. She had come to realize and accept the fact that the audit was hopelessly behind schedule and that she could do very little to clear the large number of unresolved issues for the major accounts without any meaningful help or support from Wilmeth or Kellis.

"What about investments? Are you getting closer to finishing that file? I would like to at least spend an hour on it before Kellis reviews it."

"I hope this doesn't sound like a lame excuse, Emma, but I have been basically working nonstop with the staff accountants. I have to break away sometime and try to wrap up both investments and long-term debt."

Without warning, Nelson changed the subject away from the hapless status of the BRIC audit.

"Speaking of Valentine's Day," Nelson said slyly as she looked up from her laptop, "what do you have planned tonight?"

"Well, I'll probably go home tonight and do something exciting, like watching the Discovery Channel," Bishop said as he switched on his laptop computer. "Maybe they will be showing the annual wildebeest migration on the Serengeti. Or I might catch up on the *Amish Mafia*. I've heard that's must-watch TV."

"Did you know that this is going to be my first Valentine's Day since I was a freshman in high school that I haven't had a date?"

"Oh really," Bishop said absent-mindedly without giving Nelson's statement any serious thought.

"Okay, Bishop. Here's the deal." Nelson only referred to Bishop by his last name when she was in a playful mode—which was not very often. "Forty years from now, when my husband takes me out for Valentine's Day, I want to be able to tell him that my winning streak is up to fifty years. That's not going to happen unless someone on this team steps up and takes me out tonight."

Nelson massaged her chin with the fingertips of her left hand as if she was deep in thought. By this point, she had Bishop's full attention.

"Let's see. The only viable candidates for this mission are James Wilmeth, Jackson Coleman ... and you! Guess what? Pretty much by default, you're going to have to step up and take one for the team."

Bishop leaned back in his chair and laughed softly. "Wow, if I had known this, I might have called in today with the Hong Kong flu or chronic fatigue syndrome or whatever."

"Too late for that, fella. You have been officially collared by the boss."

"Okay. Okay. Where do you want to go tonight?"

"Oh no you don't. That's your job," Nelson said as she scooped her curls off her forehead with her left hand. "You have to pick the place. Don't spoil this for me."

"Huh-oh. I can see that I am going to be stopping by a florist shop tonight. I'm sure your night would be wrecked if you didn't receive a bouquet on Valentine's Day."

"Now, that's the spirit," Nelson replied energetically. "Michael, I am surprised that you can be trained so easily. One of these years you are going to make that cute little blonde down the hall a fine husband."

10:50 a.m.

Nelson glanced at her cell phone a few moments after it began ringing.

"It's Kellis," she said with a frown.

After the conversation ended, Nelson tossed her phone back into her purse.

"Kellis wants—to use his words—a 'complete, thorough, no-holds-barred' report on exactly where we are on the BRIC audit. Before he and Wilmeth show up here at two this afternoon, he wants me to come up with a schedule of all audit adjustments that have been proposed or will likely be proposed."

"Was he upset?" Bishop asked.

"He wasn't happy."

Bishop guessed that Kellis's sudden interest in the BRIC audit had been prompted by a blunt inquiry from Suzanne Jennings regarding the status of the audit.

"Well, we need to get to work." Nelson stood as she peered over her shoulder at the large audit trunk near the entrance of the conference room that contained hard copies of the lead schedules for each of the accounts being audited. "I will make a list of all of the accounts and then we can sit down together and do our best to come up with some off-the-wall number for each one of them."

"Okay, let's do it," Bishop replied in a supportive tone.

1:20 p.m.

Bud Wallace's face was flushed and he was short of breath as he rushed into the audit conference room without pausing at the door to excuse himself.

"Michael. I need to speak with you."

Bishop glanced at Nelson and then got up and followed Wallace out of the conference room.

Rather than taking Bishop to his office, Wallace led him to an isolated corner of the employee break room.

"We have a big problem. Jennings just told me that she is going to issue the earnings press release at 10 a.m. this coming Monday morning, a week ahead of schedule. She has already contacted the securities analysts and made arrangements to do a webcast with them shortly after the earnings report is released." Wallace struggled to catch his breath. "She told me to fudge revenues again by backdating some January sales because now she has decided that the fourth-quarter number should be sixty-one cents a share. That is two cents more than the pre-audit number and three cents more than the consensus earnings forecast for the quarter. This is the worst part. She told me that she is going to force Kellis to go along with her number. She told me verbatim that she has him 'wrapped around her little finger.'" Wallace stepped forward and whispered, "What are we going to do?"

As Wallace was speaking, Bishop realized that Jennings was likely trying to rush Kellis into signing off on the fourth-quarter earnings figure before he had sufficient time to review the audit work papers and investigate any major problems that the audit team had uncovered. Jennings knew that if Kellis approved her earnings number, it would be difficult for him to subsequently retract that approval.

"What about your plan?" Bishop asked as he backed away from Wallace. "You are supposed to leak the information regarding that big inventory overstatement to us."

"I was going to do that next Wednesday, but I don't have all of the hard numbers that I need right now." Wallace was on the verge of hyperventilating.

"Okay. Calm down. Exactly what is your plan," Bishop asked.

Wallace took a deep breath and then gathered his thoughts. "Instead of just focusing on inventory, I came up with what I think is a better idea. The Molds and Dies Division has an entire product line that is now obsolete. One of our major competitors came up with a series of new engineering specifications for that same product line but hasn't gone public with that information yet. Their new product line will make our competing products obsolete. So, we will have to reverse-engineer their new products and retool our production line, which will take at least twelve months. We are looking at a significant restructuring charge for the shutdown of the product line and the re-tooling. A big piece of that will be an inventory write-down. Altogether, the restructuring charge should shave at least twenty to twenty-five cents off the fourth-quarter earnings number. You and I can sit down and come up with a strategy to 'accidentally' leak this information to your audit team."

"So, is Jennings aware of this?" Bishop asked.

"Of course she is." Wallace was upset by Bishop's naive question. "We have been keeping it under wraps for the past couple of months. Jennings doesn't want this information to get out before the deal with the private equity firm is closed."

"This doesn't make any sense," Bishop responded. "Why wouldn't the competitor go public with that information?"

"Man, are you dense?" a now wild-eyed Wallace asked. "The competitor's two senior executives and Hakes, Zimmer, and Jennings all worked together at an East Coast consulting firm. Those two guys each have a large block of BRIC stock and don't want to take a bath on it. They intend to bail out of the stock as soon as the news of the takeover by the private equity firm hits the street and causes a big run-up in our stock price. All of these SOBs may be working for competing companies, but on the side they are all balled up together looking out for their mutual interests instead of the interests of their stockholders."

Bishop had no idea whether to believe Wallace and his fanciful story. He also had no idea that Wallace's story would soon become even more shocking.

"I don't like this at all," Bishop said. "You know how soft restructuring charges are. Plus, how are you going to make a case for this in just two days? Especially if the competitor's top executives are going to cover for Hakes, Zimmer, and Jennings?"

"Listen Bishop, none of this should matter anyway. You don't even need the restructuring charge. If you guys are doing your job, you should have more than enough adjusting entries to easily cut that sixty-one cent earnings number in half, if not more. Hell, we have tampered with every number on the P&L statement from sales all the way down to taxes." Wallace stepped closer to Bishop. "You have to do something. You have to insist to Kellis that he can't sign off on Jennings' earnings number and let her issue that earnings press release."

Instead of responding, Bishop stepped away from Wallace and gazed out a window at the crowded city streets nine stories below.

"Listen," Wallace said frantically as he reached out and grabbed Bishop's right arm. "The two of us are in this together. If this doesn't work out, we both may wind up dead."

"What are you talking about?" Bishop asked incredulously as he spun around to face Wallace.

"Dammit, Bishop. The feds caught me red-handed running a pump and dump scheme four years ago. Because they had already caught me selling worthless securities down in Florida a few years before that, I only had two choices. Cooperate with their plan to try to take down the Agency or go to jail." Wallace gritted his teeth before continuing. "They set me up with some fake credentials and reference letters and got me this job at BRIC Industries just as the board was negotiating to hire the new management team of Jennings and her two buddies." Wallace shook his head in disgust. "I've had to spend three-plus years in this hellhole while all of this came together."

"Wait a minute," Bishop said breathlessly. "You are working with the feds in double-crossing the Agency?"

"Yes, dammit. Just like you. The Agency approached me more than a year ago, just like the feds thought they would, given my prior history."

Bishop's pulse was now racing uncontrollably.

"Have you known all along that I was working with the feds?" Bishop whispered.

"No. I just found out three days ago. A rookie agent with the FBI spilled the beans accidentally. I had no idea you were working with the feds. You did a damn good job of convincing me that you were freelancing on your own."

Bishop stood staring at Wallace, too stunned to respond.

"Hear me out." Wallace poked his right index finger into Bishop's chest before continuing. "We have got to make this come off. Whatever it takes. Again, it's me and you against the feds and the Agency. Like I said, if we don't pull this off and the Agency finds out that we double-crossed them, we're going to be dead meat. You think that someone in that organization wouldn't have us whacked for a few hundred dollars if we cost them fifty or sixty million?"

"But the FBI said that the Agency wasn't violent," Bishop replied as he slapped away Wallace's hand.

"You actually fell for that line from the feds? Those guys are the masters of misinformation and misdirection. They stare you straight in the eye and then tell you what they want you to believe regardless of whether it's the truth or not." Wallace shook his head in disbelief at Bishop's naivete. "And don't think the feds are looking out for you and me. Those SOBs are more cold-blooded than the Agency guys. Some of those Agency guys actually believe that they are some kind of public service organization that is cleaning up the stock market. In fact, I'll bet anything that Mal fed you that line the other night."

Wallace checked his surroundings for the third time in the past few minutes to make sure that no one was within earshot. "But that doesn't mean that someone in that organization wouldn't snuff both of us out if they found out that we were double-crossing them. If we got taken out, that would just be what the feds call 'collateral damage.' No big deal," Wallace said mimicking one of the stern-faced FBI agents. "They will find another crook to replace me and there are lots of red-blooded All-American types like you who will swallow hook, line, and sinker their patriotic line of b.s."

"Why should I believe any word that is coming out of your mouth?" Bishop asked angrily.

"What incentive do I have to lie to you about all of this?" Wallace shot back as he briefly raised his voice.

"This is all crap. This could have been dealt with in so many ways without going through all of this craziness."

"The fault all lies with the feds. We were planning to do this back in the third quarter when Jennings was out of town," Wallace explained. "But the earnings miss wasn't big enough and those press releases that Hakes and Zimmer sent out caused the stock price to recover quickly. The feds then insisted on dragging this out for several more months because they stumbled upon some information back in late October that they thought was going to allow them to do a better job of pinpointing exactly which BRIC short sellers were tied to the Agency. They put me in a huge bind because I had to do everything I could to get the Agency to allow me to hold off until we released the fourth-quarter results to get the stock price down."

Wallace again shot furtive glances over each of his shoulders. "The feds came up with the idea of convincing you to cooperate with me by feeding you that lame sob story about my father. They were afraid that Kellis might roll over and refuse to force Jennings to report a bad earnings number for the fourth quarter. That forced me to sell the Agency on the idea of getting you involved in all of this. Someone in the organization insisted on setting up a meeting to let Charles and Zed check you out." Wallace shook his head in anger. "It was also the feds who came up with the bright idea of me hooking up with Nelson. They were more than hacked off when I couldn't make that work."

"Can't you just somehow leak the information regarding BRIC's actual earnings for the fourth quarter?"

"No way. If something went wrong, I would wind up having the feds and the Agency down on my neck. The feds want to minimize the chance of any big headlines alleging an accounting fraud in this case that might result in their ongoing investigation of the Agency being compromised. And the Agency sure as hell doesn't want to have any big criminal investigation in this particular case because they went overboard and took a much larger short position in the company's stock than normal. If there is a criminal investigation, you can be damn sure that they would consider taking us both out just to shut us up."

Wallace took a deep breath. "You damn auditors can do this quietly and effectively. You can just report that you found some accounting 'errors' that had to be corrected. That wouldn't draw a huge amount of attention to all of this, but it would cause BRIC's stock price to fall out of bed. Your firm sure as hell has an incentive to avoid revealing that BRIC was engaging in a long-term fraud because that would almost force the PCAOB to investigate your prior BRIC audits."

Bishop stepped around Wallace and began to walk away. As he did, Wallace reached out and grabbed his left arm. "Whatever you do, Bishop, don't tell the feds that I told you all of this. After I found out that you were working with them, I promised them that I wouldn't tell you."

"Whatever," Bishop muttered as he jerked his arm away

"What's your plan, Bishop? We have to work together, dammit."

Bishop ignored Wallace as he turned and headed toward the nearest exit of the break room.

1:35 p.m.

As Bishop walked down the hallway in the direction of the audit conference room, he looked over his shoulder to make sure that Wallace wasn't in view and then turned to his right toward a bank of elevators. Within a couple of minutes, he was in Tanner White's former office calling the FBI on his secure cell phone.

When Jake answered, Bishop told him about the startling revelations that Bud Wallace had just made.

"That damn snitch," Jake replied. "I knew all along that we couldn't trust that crook."

"So, what he said is all true?"

"Yes," Jake replied matter-of-factly.

"Why didn't you tell me that he was working with you guys?"

"That should be obvious." For the first time, there was no hint of empathy in Jake's voice as he spoke to Bishop. "We had to make sure that neither one of you was double-crossing us. Each of you served as a check against the other."

"So, you never trusted me?"

"Listen, Bishop, we aren't in the trusting business. You of all people, an independent auditor who is paid to be skeptical, should appreciate that."

Jake paused for a moment before continuing.

"Bishop, Wayne is on the line with us now. He has something he wants to ask you."

"Hello Michael. So what do you think about the idea of the restructuring charge that Wallace came up with?" Wayne asked. "Do you think that charge would be enough to convince Kellis to back Jennings off her earnings number of sixty-one cents per share?"

Bishop hesitated for several moments to calm down and to gain control over his emotions, the primary one being the resentment that he now felt toward the FBI agents.

"I'm not sure. But … I don't like the idea," Bishop said. "If you know anything about restructuring charges, you know that they are very soft numbers. They are very subjective and hard to nail down. Plus, I have no idea whether—"

"Just a minute, Michael," Wayne said as he cut off Bishop. "I am going to put you on hold while I speak to Jake."

As the moments passed, Bishop became increasingly anxious as he wondered what the two agents were discussing. Finally, they returned to the line.

"Michael, looks like we have to go with Plan B," Wayne said decisively. "You will have to play this by ear. Whatever you have to do to keep Kellis from caving in to Jennings, then do it. That may mean threatening to call the office managing partner, your firm's headquarters office, or something even more drastic. We can't allow BRIC to issue a favorable number for the fourth quarter."

Bishop's only response was a silent shake of his head.

"Hey Bishop. This is Jake again. Uh, Michael, do you think that you could somehow persuade either Nelson or Wilmeth to stiffen up and take on Kellis?"

Bishop cleared his throat before he spoke. "Well, I guess I can try that route. But I don't think that it is going to work."

"Here's the deal," Jake responded. "If you have to butt heads with Kellis, then you're public accounting career is probably over. We don't want that because we think you could be extremely valuable to us if you stayed with your employer. So, if there is any way you can stay on the sidelines, so to speak, take that route. But, again, the number one priority is that Jennings has to back off her number and agree to release a disappointing earnings report for the fourth quarter. Do you understand that?"

"Yes. I understand."

"Okay then. You have your marching orders," Jake said gruffly. "Keep us informed. Call us anytime, even in the middle of the night."

1:55 p.m.

As Bishop entered the audit conference room, Emma Nelson glanced at her wristwatch. "Michael, you have been gone more than thirty minutes. What is going on? Kellis and Wilmeth should be here any minute and I need your help."

"Emma. I'm sorry. But, uh, I have been with Wallace all this time. We … well … we have another problem."

For the next few minutes, Bishop told Nelson of his meeting with the frantic Wallace, carefully editing the information that Wallace had given him. The primary information he conveyed to her was the large restructuring charge that BRIC needed to record. He also told her that Jennings insisted on ignoring that restructuring charge and reporting $.61 per share as the earning figure for the fourth quarter.

"I think Wallace told me about the restructuring charge because he has gotten very nervous about all the accounting shenanigans that are going on here." Bishop was able to remain calm and collected as he delivered the unsettling news to Nelson although inwardly he was struggling to maintain control over the wide range of emotions that he was experiencing. "I think we have both known for quite a while that this management team is doing everything possible to window dress BRIC's financial statements. And the reason is obvious. They want to sell this company down the river to that private equity firm."

When Bishop finished, Nelson leaned back in her chair and began twirling one of her long blonde curls around her right index finger as she often did when she was stressed.

"What do you think we should do, Michael?" The tone of her voice was deferential, signaling that she would be relying on Bishop's judgment rather than her own.

"There is only one thing to do, Emma." Bishop who had been avoiding Nelson's gaze forced himself to face her. "I think you have to tell Kellis that there is no way that we can sign off on that number that Jennings wants to report. If you don't, then the buyout deal will go forward. I think BRIC's management is betting that all of the fudging of the accounting numbers will be difficult for the new owners to unwind. It will probably take months for the new owners to even begin to realize that they have been duped. And then, it will take a lot longer, if ever, for them to actually prove it." Bishop paused as he turned away from Nelson. "But, the fact of the matter is, we know that the numbers are wrong and we should … we have to … do what is right."

Nelson picked up a pencil and began slowly tapping it on the tabletop. "Michael, I trust you and your judgment more than anyone associated with this crazy audit."

"Thanks, Emma." Bishop tried to stifle his guilt before attempting to once more persuade her to face off with Kellis. "I'm afraid that unless someone puts pressure on Kellis, he may go along with whatever Suzanne Jennings wants to do."

There is no doubt in my mind that she is behind all of the accounting gimmicks. I think that Wallace and all the others are just her gofers."

Nelson stared into space for several moments before turning her attention back to Bishop.

"You're right all around, Michael, including about Suzanne Jennings. That's hard for me to admit because I looked up to her so much." Nelson paused to strengthen her resolve. "It is my responsibility to bring this up with Kellis. And I will do it. It is the right thing to do; it's the only thing to do."

2:45 p.m.

At a quarter till three, Suzanne Jennings barged unannounced into the audit conference room.

"Where is Cason Kellis?" Jennings asked harshly as she stood peering at Nelson with her arms crossed tightly across her chest.

"Ms. Jennings, he was supposed to arrive with Jim Wilmeth forty-five minutes ago. But, as you can see, neither of them is here."

Jennings nostrils flared as she tossed her head back and snapped, "Yes, I can 'see' that they are not here. Now, where are they?"

"Ma'am, I don't know. In fact, you have probably spoken to one or both of them since I have."

Nelson had no intention of inflaming Jennings and instead was simply trying to respond to her as fully and politely as possible. Jennings, though, had a different interpretation of Nelson's statements.

"Young lady, do not be rude to me. I happen to be the chief financial officer of this company, if you haven't heard." Before giving the shell-shocked Nelson a chance to respond, Jennings did a pirouette and stormed out of the conference room.

3:10 p.m.

When Cason Kellis arrived at the audit conference room with Jim Wilmeth in tow, Emma Nelson immediately told him that Suzanne Jennings wanted to speak to him.

"Great. Just terrific," Kellis spat in disgust. "When was she here?"

"Exactly twenty-five minutes ago," Nelson responded after checking her wristwatch.

Kellis was angry and distraught while Wilmeth was grim and seemingly disinterested. It was readily apparent to Bishop that there was enormous tension between the two men. Most likely, Wilmeth had told Kellis that the BRIC audit was nowhere near complete and that the company's accounting records were laced with misstatements. Those factual observations had likely prompted a quarrel between them regarding how to resolve the emerging crisis triggered by Suzanne Jennings' decision to report an impressive fourth-quarter earnings number the following Monday.

After ripping off his suit jacket and throwing it to the far end of the conference room table, Kellis pulled out his cell phone and called Jennings' secretary and cordially told her that he would drop by Jennings' office within five minutes. Once he got off the phone, Dr. Jekyll reverted to Mr. Hyde.

"Okay. Where's that schedule of audit adjustments," Kellis barked at Nelson. Bishop had never witnessed Kellis speak to Nelson in that manner.

After scanning the one-page schedule, Kellis threw it down on the table. "Bishop, close that door."

Despite being offended by Kellis's demeaning tone, Bishop got up and casually closed the conference room door. Before he settled back down in his seat, Kellis had begun ranting.

"Okay, here's the deal. I'm going down to Jennings' office. When I get back, someone is going to walk me through each of these accounts. Inventory, receivables, payables, revenues, and so on. Whoever is the most knowledgeable for any given account, that's who I want to take the lead for that account. I want to know everything that I need to know to determine exactly how firm these audit adjustments are." Kellis stopped and placed his hands on his hips. "I want to know which of these adjustments are absolutely necessary and the down-to-the-bone minimum adjustment that we can accept for each account."

Kellis headed toward the conference room door and then abruptly wheeled and faced his subordinates once more. "Understand this. I am not interested in dollars or millions of dollars. I am interested in one thing. I want to know how many pennies, if any—hopefully none—that have to be sliced off the sixty-one cents a share that Jennings intends to report as earnings for the fourth quarter." Kellis glanced at each of his three subordinates in turn. "Every one of those pennies is sacred to that woman. If someone wants to make a major dent in that sixty-one cent figure, then that person is going with me to deliver the news to that hellion."

Kellis jerked open the door to the conference room, but then spun around again. This time he addressed Nelson only. "I want you to tell everyone on the audit team that Valentine's Day has been cancelled and that, if necessary, we will be here all night."

3:45 p.m.

After Cason Kellis left, Jim Wilmeth reluctantly told Nelson and Bishop to take a seat on either side of him. For the next 30 minutes, until Kellis returned to the conference room, Wilmeth questioned Nelson and Bishop about each account listed on the schedule. Although Kellis had referred to them as "audit adjustments," the amounts on the schedule were no more than guesstimates prepared by Nelson and Bishop since most of the work paper files were incomplete and lacked a formal estimate of any audit adjustment that was necessary. The two seniors had not taken the time to add the amounts; but, if they had, the total would have easily wiped out BRIC's pre-audit net income for the fourth quarter.

When Kellis returned, he was no longer hyperkinetic and histrionic, but he was still enormously upset.

"Give me that damn schedule," he said to Wilmeth as he took a seat on the other side of the table from his three subordinates.

After studying the schedule for several minutes without speaking, Kellis looked at Wilmeth. "How long would it take you to go back and update all of the work paper files that have any reference to the materiality limits that you and I established at the beginning of the audit?"

Instead of responding, Wilmeth yawned as he leaned back in his chair and stared at the door of the conference room while avoiding eye contact with the audit partner.

"Hey, I asked you a question," Kellis snapped. "Do you want me to repeat it?"

"No. That's alright. I heard you the first time," Wilmeth replied calmly without looking at Kellis.

Several more tension-packed moments passed before Wilmeth turned and faced Kellis.

"Listen, if you have the crazy ____ idea of going back and changing all the materiality limits, then you can either do it yourself or get one of your gofers here to do it for you. There is no way in hell that I'm going to be involved in that."

"That's insubordination, dammit," Kellis growled. "That's grounds for immediate dismissal."

Wilmeth leaned forward and then spoke through clenched teeth. "You listen to me. I know you were the ____ that told Wilson to get rid of me. So go ___ ___."

Kellis was visibly shocked by both the hate-filled tone of Wilmeth's voice and the expletives he had spoken. Before he could collect his thoughts and reply, Wilmeth spoke again.

"You must be dumber than I thought. You're the one that needs me. Not vice versa. If this thing blows up, I'm blaming it all on you. And I have the facts to back me up."

Nelson and Bishop sat silently as they took in the melodrama playing out before them. "Now," Wilmeth continued, "I don't know why I am doing this, but I am going to do you a favor. You are going to take those adjustments down to

Jennings and tell her that she has to book every damn last one of them. You're not going to enjoy it, Slick, but you are going to do it. And it's very likely going to save your career. If this blows up and there is an SEC investigation, followed by the PCAOB sending a squad of their head-knockers out here, it's very likely that your career is going to be finished. Once they get through with you, you and Katy will be moving out of that mansion on the golf course and buying a tu-tone double-wide to park in a cow pasture somewhere."

It was readily apparent that Kellis absorbed and processed every one of Wilmeth's stinging words. After Wilmeth finished his harangue, Kellis leaned back in his chair and took a deep breath. A few moments later, Nelson broke the silence.

"I have to agree with Jim. There's no denying that this client is doing everything it can to intentionally overstate its earnings. And, now, we have found out from Wallace that a major restructuring charge is necessary. If we—"

Kellis viciously slapped the surface of the conference room table with his right hand, cutting off Nelson in mid-sentence. "Who asked you for your damn input?" he shouted.

"You did," Nelson shouted back, "when you agreed to have me to supervise the fieldwork."

"That was my first damn mistake," Kellis shot back. "I should have put someone in charge out here who knew how to run an audit."

Bishop assumed that Nelson would become emotional and back down. He was wrong.

"I did the very best I could out here," the suddenly fiery and resilient Nelson responded. "We all did. You threw us out here without sufficient resources or supervision to do this job and you know it. I have been trying to tell you for weeks that this audit was in trouble, but you refused to listen."

"I have no memory of that whatsoever." The tone of Kellis's voice revealed that he was blatantly lying to protect himself.

Before Nelson had a chance to respond, Kellis got to his feet and turned his back on her and his two other subordinates and then stood with his hands on his hips facing the closed conference room door.

After a lengthy pause, Kellis turned around and addressed Wilmeth. "You can go back to the office now." Kellis's words were civil but his voice was quaking with rage. "Go back to work on that hospital engagement."

Wilmeth slowly rose to his feet, picked up his satchel, and then left the conference room without saying a word.

A short time later, Kellis looked at Nelson as he prepared to leave the conference room. "Until we are finished on this job, I want everyone to put in twelve-plus chargeable hours each day, seven days a week. Is that understood?"

"Sure thing, Boss," Nelson replied caustically as she stared down Kellis.

6:55 p.m.

Shortly before 7 p.m., Kellis returned to the conference room with Todd Wilson, the OMP. Wilson was a short, wiry man in his late fifties with a surprisingly deep voice that resonated with a ring of judicial authority each time that he spoke. After brusquely introducing Nelson and Bishop to Wilson, Kellis asked Nelson for the "schedule of audit adjustments."

Wilson and Kellis sat down at the far end of conference room table and studied the one-page schedule for ten minutes or more. As they did, they occasionally spoke to each other in a muffled tone to prevent Nelson and Bishop from making out what they were saying. Finally, Wilson began asking questions of Nelson. The thrust of most of the questions focused on how "firm" or "reliable" the given "adjustments" were. Nelson attempted to refer one of Wilson's first few questions to Bishop, but Wilson would have none of it.

"Young lady, as I understand it, you are the supervising audit senior. You are in charge of the fieldwork. You are the one who has to accept responsibility for that fieldwork. So, I want you to respond, not your subordinate."

A properly chastised Nelson accepted Wilson's admonition and from that point on did the best job she could of explaining and defending the items listed on the schedule. Despite her courage under fire, Nelson stumbled through her responses. Wilson did not attempt to hide his contempt or displeasure at her lightweight and often contradictory summaries of the given items.

Once Wilson was done interrogating Nelson, he paused and turned to Kellis. The two partners exchanged disapproving frowns. Wilson seemed to be conveying to Kellis that everything that Kellis had previously told him about Nelson— whatever that was—was true.

Wilson then turned back to Nelson. He asked her about her relationship with Jim Wilmeth and how they had gotten along. Then, he asked her whether Wilmeth had seemed "invested" in the BRIC audit. Finally, he asked her if she had ever witnessed Wilmeth working on the hospital audit while in the BRIC audit conference room.

Nelson answered each of Wilson's questions honestly. As she was replying to the series of questions, Bishop realized what was happening. Kellis and Wilson were going to blame the disastrous BRIC audit on Wilmeth's inattention and Nelson's incompetence.

Once Wilson had finished questioning Nelson for the second time, he turned to Kellis. "Cason, it is time for us to make that promised visit to Suzanne. Are you up for it?"

Kellis nodded affirmatively.

Wilson instructed Nelson and Bishop to continue working on their assignments "as normal." He also told them that he and Kellis would return after speaking with Jennings, although he wasn't sure how long that would be. "In the meantime, please let each of the staff accountants know that they can go home," Wilson said to Nelson before he and Kellis left the conference room.

10:05 p.m.

For more than two hours, Nelson and Bishop sat working in the audit conference room without speaking or making eye contact with each other.

When Wilson and Kellis returned to the conference room a few minutes after 10 p.m., they both looked emotionally drained. After sitting down at the conference room table, Wilson addressed Nelson.

"Miss Nelson, you have had a long, long day and an even longer week. Why don't you go on home. In fact, I want you to sleep in tomorrow morning. Just show up whenever you feel like it. Hopefully before lunch," he added with a forced laugh.

Nelson gathered her personal effects and then silently mouthed the words "good bye" as she looked at Bishop on her way out of the conference room.

After Nelson left, Wilson apologized to Bishop for the late hour. "Michael, I hate to keep you here any longer since it is past ten o'clock, but I need to speak to you."

Over the next 20 minutes, Wilson briefed Bishop on what had transpired over the previous several hours and what was to come on the BRIC audit. All the while, a subdued and downcast Cason Kellis sat idly beside Wilson, directly across the table from Bishop.

Wilson explained that Suzanne Jennings had agreed to postpone BRIC's earnings press release. The press release had been tentatively rescheduled for Friday, February 28, shortly before the company filed its Form 10-K with the SEC. Wilson said the actual earnings figure reported by BRIC would be determined over the following two weeks but that it would be a "very disappointing" figure for the company. If it was not possible to get a "good handle" on BRIC's fourth-quarter earnings number or if it was deemed necessary to restate any of the earnings reports for the first three quarters of the year, the earnings press release and the filing of BRIC's 10-K with the SEC would be delayed "as long as necessary."

"Michael, this will be our last audit of this company. For that reason, we want the work papers to be as clean as possible. And we want to make sure that the final proposed audit adjustments are conservative. That is, if there is any doubt, we want you to lean toward overstating the proposed adjustment for any given expense account, for example, rather than understating the adjustment."

Wilson leaned over and whispered something to Kellis. After a few more whispered exchanges between the two men, Wilson turned back to Bishop.

"We want you to take the lead in cleaning up the work papers. By 'cleaning up,' I mean making sure they are well organized and properly dated, that all the supporting schedules tie back to the lead schedules, that the rationale for each audit adjustment is well thought out and documented, that there are proper references to authoritative standards, if necessary, and so on and so forth."

Wilson paused as if he was selecting his next words very carefully.

"I was very impressed with your work that I have reviewed, Michael, and I want you to know that Cason and I appreciate your dedication and professionalism under less than ideal circumstances. We have no doubt that you can handle this assignment that we are giving you. Having said that, we are going to assign an audit manager to help you."

"Oh yes," Wilson said after Kellis whispered something in his ear. "We also want you to take the lead in redrafting the ICFR memo. Miss Henderson has written an initial draft of that memo, but, quite frankly, we believe that the memo should be completely rewritten. Based upon a brief review of the internal control tests results and the results of the year-end substantive tests, Cason and I believe there are multiple material weaknesses in BRIC's internal controls over financial reporting that must be documented in the ICFR memo. Of course, that means an adverse opinion will have to be included in the memo."

Wilson turned to Kellis and asked him the name of the audit manager who would be replacing Jim Wilmeth.

"Cassie Suarez," Kellis replied.

"That's right. Her name had slipped my mind with everything going on," Wilson said before focusing his attention back on Bishop. "Cassie is a newly promoted audit manager who just wrapped up an audit on a client that has one of those rare November 30 year-ends. She is not going to be well versed with respect to this client, but she can give you guidance in terms of the wrap-up procedures for an audit, including polishing up the work papers, archiving them and so on. Understand that Miss Nelson will remain on the engagement. However, we want the two of you to swap roles. You will be the supervising audit senior and she will be assisting you."

Wilson paused to collect his thoughts again. "You can understand that this is an unusual set of circumstances. I know that you and Miss Suarez, and Miss Nelson, for that matter, will handle the situation professionally."

Wilson glanced at Kellis, signaling a change in the topic of conversation.

"There are a few other topics that Cason wants to discuss with you, but I am going to head home now. Hopefully, the two of you can wrap everything up in a few minutes and get out of here," Wilson said with a tired but genuine smile. "And, by the way, I don't want you to be here at seven or eight in the morning either. If you insist, you can roll in at ten or eleven, but feel free to show up after lunch if you want." Wilson stood and reached across the table. "Thank you again, Michael," he said as he firmly shook Bishop's hand.

"Cason, I will speak to you first thing Monday morning," Wilson said to Kellis before leaving the conference room.

After Wilson left, Kellis spent several moments flipping through pages of scribbled notes on a yellow legal pad that he had brought with him when he returned to the conference room.

"Michael, as you can understand, Suzanne Jennings is less than happy that BRIC Industries will not be reporting the earnings number that she wants for the fourth quarter." Kellis managed a weak smile as he added, "She made the insults that Jim Wilmeth sent my way seem like flattering tributes. And let's just say that Sam Hakes and Jett Zimmer won't be inviting me to play golf again anytime soon." For the first time in Bishop's presence, Kellis was low key and respectful, treating him as a fellow professional rather than as a subordinate.

"As you probably gathered from what Todd said, our firm will be dismissed as BRIC's auditor following the completion of this audit. Todd and I are both concerned that there may be litigation stemming from this situation. If that happens, it wouldn't surprise either one of us if the SEC steps in and investigates this company. There's also a good chance that the PCAOB might investigate this audit and the prior audits at the same time. That is why we want you to remain here with Cassie Suarez as long as necessary to get the work papers in tip-top shape. We are going to leave Jackson Coleman and Becky Linton here to help you along with two rookie staff accountants, but Emma Nelson will likely leave after two or three more weeks."

Kellis paused and took a deep breath before continuing. "There is no doubt that this audit was destined for failure from the beginning. Jim Wilmeth clearly failed to carry out his responsibilities as the audit manager. And, in hindsight, Emma Nelson was obviously not qualified to supervise the fieldwork."

Kellis again flipped through the scribbled notes on his yellow legal pad.

"I just want to make sure that you and I are in agreement regarding what happened here. There is no doubt that you are a fine auditor and that you understand that the two of us will need to work together to ... uh ... uh ..." Kellis was struggling to find the proper words to convey his thoughts. "What I am trying to say is that this situation will likely drag on for quite some time, probably for several years. I want you to look at this as an opportunity. You can use this unfortunate set of circumstances as a springboard to better things. In fact, I have already asked Todd Wilson that you be assigned to the biotech audit team that I am assembling."

Kellis hesitated to backtrack momentarily.

"You probably haven't heard that we have picked up two major biotech companies that we had been pursuing as audit clients the past several months. That's confidential information, by the way. But it does mean that we can forge ahead with creating the biotech service team for our office, which I will head up. We are going to assign only top-notch young men and women to that team. So, you should be proud of being selected. You will not only learn a lot about that incredible line of business, but I will also mentor you and do my best to promote your career with the firm."

Kellis took off his bow tie and tossed it on the table as he once again searched for the precise words that he wanted to use.

"You know, Michael, first and foremost, auditing is a business. And the business world is all about, uh, you know, making alliances. Mutually supportive alliances."

Kellis fiddled nervously with a pen lying on the table in front of him.

"Let me stop there. What are your thoughts? Do you understand … what I am … I mean … do you have any questions?"

It was obvious to Bishop that Cason Kellis had just laid a *quid pro quo* contract on the table: Kellis would promote Bishop's career, if Bishop made a commitment to "cover" for Kellis in the future if the BRIC audit came under intense scrutiny. Bishop realized that if he accepted Kellis's offer, he was agreeing to throw Jim Wilmeth and Emma Nelson under the bus and blame them for the BRIC audit fiasco while defending Kellis's role on the audit. But, unlike Kellis, Bishop knew that it was very unlikely that the BRIC audit would ever come under intense scrutiny, at least by the PCAOB or any other federal regulatory authorities.

Once more, Michael Bishop faced one of those life-changing decisions that his grandmother had spoken to him about years earlier. He realized that both the FBI and the Agency would want him to accept Kellis's loathsome offer. But because BRIC Industries would be reporting a disappointing earnings number for the fourth quarter, he felt he had accomplished the primary objective that each had given him. So, in his mind, he was free to choose. He could choose the schizophrenic lifestyle in which he secretly cooperated with the FBI and the Agency while he served as Cason Kellis's wingman and newest BFF. Or he could choose to walk away and find another job, a job that would allow him return to the humdrum, monotonous lifestyle that he had known before his meeting with Bud Wallace in the Grotto.

As he sat there staring intently at Kellis who was becoming more nervous and uncomfortable with each passing moment, Bishop felt an unexpected surge of adrenaline. It suddenly occurred to him that not only did he have the ability to choose his future, he was truly needed by the FBI, and he was desperately needed by Kellis. He enjoyed the feeling of being in control of his future and of being needed. It made him feel powerful. That was a good thing.

"I'm happy that you have so much confidence in me," Bishop said in a strong and resolute tone as he stared directly into Kellis's eyes. "I would very much like to join the biotech team and work closely with you. And I understand exactly what you are suggesting in terms of us working together in the future when issues arise regarding this audit."

Bishop's facial expression communicated more than his words to Kellis. When the audit partner realized that Bishop had "signed off" on the mutually beneficial contract that he had offered him, he smiled broadly and gave Bishop a reassuring wink.

Epilogue

Michael Bishop took a seat on one of the benches halfway down the Seal Beach pier and then leaned back and adjusted his sunglasses. He was decked out in a patriotic t-shirt, cargo shorts, and sandals. It was July 4th and the holiday celebration was in full swing along the Orange County coastline of southern California. The popular pier was packed with happy families from Ohio and Michigan and other Midwestern outposts who were spending the holiday enjoying the perfect weather and carnival-like atmosphere of the pier.

A few days earlier, Bishop had flown to LAX where his mother and sister had met him. For three weeks, he would be vacationing in sunny southern California, the known center of the universe, at least in his mind. After his vacation, he would be spending an additional two weeks in nearby Newport Beach attending a training course that Cason Kellis had recommended. The intense in-house course was designed to acquaint participants with the key accounting and financial reporting issues faced by the burgeoning biopharmaceutical industry as well as the business models and revenue streams of biopharmaceutical companies.

Kellis had handpicked Bishop to supervise the fieldwork on the year-end audit of one of the two large biopharmaceutical companies that he had recruited as audit clients for their practice office. Before, during, and following the audit, Bishop would be working on a large consulting project that Kellis had successfully marketed to the client. The biopharmaceutical firm had gone public only two years earlier and its common stock was a darling of Wall Street. Since the company's initial public offering, its stock price had more than quadrupled despite the company having only minimal revenues and no expectations of any operating profits for at least two years.

After learning that Bishop would serve as the supervising audit senior on the biopharmaceutical company's upcoming audit, Jeremiah, Bishop's newly appointed contact person within the Agency, was thrilled. According to Jeremiah, the biopharmaceutical firm had been identified by his organization as a company that was potentially embellishing its financial and operating data in its periodic SEC reports. His organization was biding its time to decide when to begin taking short positions in the company's stock. Jeremiah told Bishop that in his role as audit senior he would be perfectly positioned to provide critical inside information that would be instrumental in making that decision.

Bishop had spent much of the previous four and one-half months working on the BRIC Industries audit. The company had been forced to delay the filing of its

Form 10-K with the SEC for more than three months. Instead of the $.61 earnings per share figure that Jennings had wanted to report for the fourth quarter, BRIC had eventually reported a loss of $.17 per share for that quarter and issued restated financial statements for the three previous quarters of the year. Those restatements had reduced BRIC's previously reported earnings by $.34 per share. The company's board had been concerned that the restatements might trigger an SEC investigation, but Bishop had learned from the FBI that the SEC would not be investigating the company. Likewise, despite Cason Kellis's enormous and ongoing fear that the BRIC audit would eventually be the subject of a PCAOB investigation, Jake had told Bishop that there was "zero chance" of that happening.

When BRIC Industries reported in late February that it would be delaying the release of its 10-K for the previous year due to "inadvertent errors discovered by BRIC's corporate accounting staff," the company's stock price had dropped by more than 40 percent in a matter of days on its way to an eventual decline of almost 70 percent. The sharp drop in the stock's price spawned rumors that a class-action lawsuit would be filed against the company and its audit firm, Bishop's employer. Jake had assured Bishop that even if such a lawsuit was eventually filed, the defendants "would quickly settle it," meaning that Bishop would not be forced to testify regarding the BRIC audit.

Three days after BRIC Industries released its delayed 10-K and the accompanying restatements of its previous quarterly financial statements, the company's board accepted the resignations of Sam Hakes, Jett Zimmer, and Suzanne Jennings. Over the following few weeks, Bud Wallace and each of the company's divisional controllers quietly resigned and left the company.

When Emma Nelson completed her work on the BRIC engagement in early March, she was asked to meet with Todd Wilson. He informed her that her services were no longer needed by the firm and that she would receive six weeks of severance pay. Wilson then wished her good luck in finding another position. Later that evening, Nelson called Bishop to tell him that she had been fired. As the conversation came to an end, a tearful Nelson told Bishop that she would miss him and hoped that someday they would have their Valentine Day's date that they had been forced to cancel.

Occasionally, Bishop peered through his dark sunglasses at the knots of tourists approaching him. Bishop was searching the crowd for "Teddy," a Los Angeles-based FBI agent. Jake had arranged for Bishop to meet Teddy on the Seal Beach pier. Teddy was assigned to an investigation involving suspicious short-selling activity in the stock of a San Diego-based biopharmaceutical company. According to Jake, several key members of that company's audit team would be attending the Newport Beach training session at the end of July. The audit manager assigned to that team was suspected of being associated with the Agency. The FBI wanted Bishop to strike up a relationship with Lesley, an attractive young lady who had served as the supervising audit senior on the most recent audit of the San Diego-based company. The FBI believed that she was emotionally vulnerable and could be the source of meaningful information regarding the audit manager, information that could not be obtained by "conventional" means.

All in all, Bishop's life was interesting, exciting, and, in many ways, out of control. He seldom had time to think of anything but his next clandestine meeting with Jeremiah or the FBI or his next social event with Cason Kellis. Over the past few months, Kellis had attempted to ingratiate himself to Bishop by inviting him to his home for firm-related gatherings, golfing excursions with key clients, and press-the-flesh sessions where Kellis was networking and recruiting new clients for the firm.

Bishop was not only Kellis's new sidekick and wingman but also an increasingly important confidant of both the Agency and the FBI. In late June, Mal had met with Bishop and thanked him for his role in ending the accounting fraud at BRIC Industries and ridding the company of the "crooks" responsible for that scheme. He also thanked Bishop for helping his organization earn a "modest profit" when BRIC's stock price plunged—the FBI estimated that "modest" profit was in the range of $70 million. Mal was convinced that Bishop's evolving relationship with Cason Kellis would pay huge dividends down the road, particularly if Kellis succeeded Todd Wilson as the OMP.

The FBI was also extremely grateful for Bishop's masterful work in navigating his way through the BRIC debacle while, at the same time, infiltrating the Agency. Over the previous month, Bishop had met on two occasions with Irv and several other senior FBI officials who had mapped out a master plan for him to follow in developing and extending his relationship with the Agency.

In late May, Bishop's mother had called him and excitedly reported that an appreciative former student of hers "who had become rich in the stock market" had paid off her mortgage. The former student, who insisted on remaining anonymous, had also established a fund to provide a four-year scholarship for Bishop's sister, Jessica, to attend UCLA.

As Bishop thought back over the previous nine months, he realized that he could never have predicted that his life would change so radically in such a short period of time. He also realized that there was no way of predicting how long the thrilling roller coaster ride would last. But, regardless how long it lasted, he was going to hang on and enjoy it. Corporate espionage had proven to be much more entertaining than Sudoku puzzles and Netflix videos.

"Michael?"

Bishop turned to his right. Standing a few feet away was a young man in his early thirties decked out in a Hawaiian shirt and dress slacks.

"Yes, that's me. You must be Teddy," Bishop replied as he got to his feet.

"That's right. I am very glad to meet you," Teddy said as he grasped Bishop's extended right hand. "I've heard so many great things about you. You have made a tremendous impression on some really important people in our organization."

"Well, thank you, Teddy. I do my best," Bishop said with a modest smile.